INVESTED LEADERSHIP

INVESTED LEADERSHIP

EMPOWER YOUR TEAM
to LEAD *with* HEART

ERIC SANCHEZ and STACIE MONAHAN

LIONCREST
PUBLISHING

INVESTED LEADERSHIP
Empower Your Team to Lead with Heart

FIRST EDITION

ISBN   978-1-5445-4721-3   *Hardcover*
       978-1-5445-4720-6   *Paperback*
       978-1-5445-4722-0   *Ebook*

To all students of leadership.

CONTENTS

INTRODUCTION

"Regard your soldiers as your children, and they will follow you into the deepest valleys; look upon them as your own beloved sons, and they will stand by you even unto death."

—SUN TZU, *THE ART OF WAR*

A sixth-century BC warlord talking about caring for people? This is considered fundamental reading in the military? Yes, and we believe *The Art of War* is also one of the best business books ever written. The quote above always jumps out at us. Loving others like your children is an intimate and all-encompassing mandate. It's very different than caring about somebody as a friend. You'd lay down your life for your child. It's a powerful decree.

Obviously, we do not recommend business leaders lay down their lives for employees. For us, the call is to be attuned to an employee's needs. It's akin to being attuned to a child's needs. If a parent saw their child sad, they'd notice, investigate the cause, and try to assist in relieving the child's sadness. Applying this same idea to the workplace, as we will in this book, is nothing short of transformative—for employees and leadership, as well as for productivity and the bottom line.

When you are attuned to your employees' needs, you can anticipate needs. You're proactive rather than reactive, which builds trust, loyalty, and mutual respect; without those, any business will eventually fall to rival warriors. There's nothing more barbaric and guttural than war, and to be successful in it, you've got to care. How to be successful in this barbaric thing called business? Care.

THERE GOES PRODUCTIVITY

In many respects, employees have taken power back from corporate America. They now dictate whether they work remotely or not. In an especially robust economy, they decide whether or not to take a salaried job at all. Workers are moving around more than ever. The turnover rate in professional services, such as law firms, in 2023 was 57 percent.[1]

People don't work only for paychecks, and the long-term success of financial incentives is largely a myth. Everyone needs to make money, of course, but compensation doesn't determine how hard employees work, or whether they stay or go. Today, people have more options than ever. Maybe they want to work from home, or for someone who gives them the flexibility to coach their kid's soccer team, or for someone who's pledged to align the company with green initiatives. Whatever the workplace needs of your employees, if those needs aren't fulfilled, it likely won't matter how

---

[1] Jefferson Hansen, "Employee Turnover Rates by Industry: Trends and Solutions," Awardco, December 16, 2024, https://www.award.co/blog/employee-turnover-rates.

much you pay in salaries. Workplace productivity will dip, and that's the best-case scenario. At worst, you'll face a revolving door of positions to fill.

Workers have an ever-increasing number of options in today's work environment—and they know it. It's never been solely about paying your employees well (or creating a destination location for them to work in replete with game rooms and massage chairs). When employees consider what motivates them to stay at a company, they ask themselves, *Do people here truly care about me?* and also, *How do they care about me?*

CARING FOR YOUR EMPLOYEES IS NO LONGER A NICE-TO-HAVE. IT'S TABLE STAKES.

This is true for everyone, but especially true for younger generations, who seek a totally different experience to prior generations. We hear an outcry for a different kind of workplace and a different kind of leadership. In our consulting practice, our clients constantly ask for advice about how to manage this younger generation. Often, the conversation focuses more on how difficult they are or their supposed lack of work ethic than it does on how current leadership can pivot and shift its culture or management style to suit the different needs, expectations, and tolerance levels of a new generation.

Younger workers are more sensitive and hold higher expectations of having emotional needs met in the workplace. They've seen the data: they know they can actually make more money if they job hop every 18 months than if they remain loyal to one employer,[2] and they know why that statistic is true—because most companies are betting employees will prefer job security over higher pay. Why would workers strike that bargain when layoffs, particularly in the tech sector, are not only common but have been soaring in the last couple of years?[3] If they won't even stay because you pay them well, they certainly won't if you don't—unless, that is, they're getting something they want in return. Employees today have specific needs, which they demand be met in exchange for reciprocal loyalty.

It's true that younger employees are realizing maybe they care more about a company's ecological responsibility, DEI position, or efforts toward gender equity and pay transparency. Such preferences are definitely reshaping the modern workplace. But it's more than that. Even when those desires are met, we still see people leave for more personal reasons: they bail when they feel leadership doesn't care about them.

It's not just younger generations. We've both left jobs in the past for similar reasons—and each took a significant pay cut to do so—because, at least in part, we felt our employers didn't truly care about us. If an employee is giving their blood, sweat, and tears, giving 110 percent, and it's not reciprocated, why the hell would they stick around? Caring for your employees is no longer a nice-to-have. It's table stakes.

2   Cameron Keng, "Employees Who Stay in Companies Longer Than Two Years Get Paid 50% Less," Forbes, June 22, 2014, https://www.forbes.com/sites/cameronkeng/ 2014/06/22/ employees-that-stay-in-companies-longer-than-2-years-get-paid-50-less.

3   "Number of Tech Employees Laid Off Worldwide from 2020 to 2024, By Quarter," Statista, January 6, 2025, https://www.statista.com/statistics/199999/worldwide-tech-layoffs-covid-19.

PEOPLE LEAVE BAD BOSSES, NOT BAD COMPANIES.

It seems like every other month, we hear a new euphemism for employee dissatisfaction: quiet quitting, toxic culture, poor engagement. Workers have realized that life is too damn short to spend twenty years slaving for a company that barely acknowledges or knows them, that would toss them aside at the drop of a hat. Members of Gen Z may not even spend one year. This generation simply doesn't feel the same desire or need to develop loyalty toward an institution—especially one that doesn't care for them. When workers sense a lack of genuine connection, it leads to unrest that may manifest not only in problems with employee retention, but in general low morale. In 2023, 50 percent of all employees were "not engaged," or quiet quitting. Nationally, unengaged or actively disengaged workers account for $1.9 trillion in lost productivity.[4]

We see it often in many of the workplaces of our clients: unhappiness, lack of production, gossip, interoffice conflict, lack of vision. Often, we are hired to fix a problem by someone who doesn't realize they are at least part of the problem.

People leave bad bosses, not bad companies. Most bosses don't start out bad, but often, managers who were once young and hungry eventually construct echo chambers around themselves. They grow out of touch with their colleagues and staff, not considering their needs and, some-

---

4   Jim Harter, "In New Workplace, U.S. Employee Engagement Stagnates," Gallup, January 23, 2024, https://www.gallup.com/workplace/608675/new-workplace-employee-engagement-stagnates.aspx.

times, not considering them much at all, outside of what they can produce. These leaders have major blind spots—hey, we all do, but it becomes a problem when one has very little self-awareness, if any at all. They're not aware that they have turned their relationships with their employees into transactional ones and, in so doing, have pushed them away. They turn to business books, speakers, and coaches for advice on how to be stronger and more effective, but either don't genuinely own the concepts or can't implement change when it comes to themselves or leadership teams.

THE FOUNDATION OF ANY SUCCESSFUL BUSINESS CULTURE IS CARING.

Worse still, some in positions of authority who've read the latest book or watched the latest TED Talk on leadership theory think it's enough to make a ham-handed gesture of care that comes off as disingenuous. It's been in vogue at conferences to include a seminar on ensuring your employees feel "safe," so leaders return to their companies and announce, "Anyone can meet with me to share concerns about the company, without fear of repercussion." The problem presents when the leader returns and simply announces that the company is a safe space, but everyone knows it's bullshit. It has the opposite effect: it demoralizes the employees. People will instead feel vulnerable and, at worst, manipulated.

We read an article recently positing the need to focus

on employee engagement because it increases retention levels. The author was pitching a variety of ways to increase employee engagement, such as social hours and safe spaces; that completely misses the point and masks the symptoms. If you really care about people, the ways to increase employee engagement will naturally follow. If you're looking for easy ways to abate turnover, aside from genuinely caring about people, you may well create the opposite effect.

Even when the leader isn't plastic, but rather isn't the sort of person around whom employees feel safe, the tactic will backfire. This doesn't mean such leaders are bad people; they're simply not aware of the lack of trust.

Bottom line: if you're experiencing high turnover, losing good people to lateral moves or less money, or witnessing a drop in productivity, it may be an indication your culture and leadership style need attention. You don't have to be everything to everyone—in fact, it's not possible. You have to implement a strategy to ensure everyone's needs are met. If you have an optimal and healthy culture, you won't have quiet quitting and low productivity. That would simply be anathema to the organization. These are goals of Invested Leadership.

THERE ARE A VARIETY OF DIFFERENT WAYS TO LEAD PEOPLE, BUT INNATELY, LEADERSHIP SHOULD BE ABOUT SOMEONE ELSE.

HOW TO CULTIVATE LOYALTY

More and more, employees want to feel genuinely cared for. This is especially the case in younger generations, but it's truly cross generational. The foundation of any successful business culture is caring. Show us a successful business culture where people don't feel cared for—we don't think it exists.

Leadership focuses on other people and making them their absolute best. Some people need ass kicking, others need inspiration, and some just need someone to be there—in fact, it can be the same person needing all three at different times or stages in their career. Further, those needs may vary based on existing or shifting life circumstances. There are a variety of different ways to lead people, but innately, leadership should be about someone else. Good leaders have the ability to bring out the very best in other people. When you or someone else on your leadership team can pause momentarily from a task to stop and genuinely consider employees and colleagues as humans with needs, you'll get more out of them.

When people feel sincerely cared for, they reward you with loyalty; they'll follow you into any battle. It is a strategic imperative to legitimately care about your people. Some leaders have always known this, while other executives are finally starting to figure it out. If you don't root your culture in authenticity, it will only have a veneer of caring. Sooner or later, the veneer comes off, people realize they've been deceived, they get mad, and, ultimately, they leave.

If you're telling yourself right now that "of course I care for my employees," double-check if that's really true or just lip service (or if your employees could interpret it that way). We see it time and time again: under the guise of caring, leaders try to manipulate staff. Consider something like "Pizza Friday." Some may mistakenly think free food will alone make a staff believe the boss is generous. That's not how it works. If you're flying private jets and then spend a few bucks on Domino's once a month, you're only drawing attention to the disparity.

On the other hand, some bosses simply don't know how their employees prefer to be cared for. That's just a blind spot. To be clear, the real problem in the pizza scenario is the disingenuousness. Blind spots can be filled. You may be genuinely unable (or simply unwilling) to care for your employees in the ways they need to be cared for, or perhaps you do not have the bandwidth. You might not even have the skillset! That's okay. That doesn't necessarily make you a bad leader. There are other ways to achieve the same goal besides putting on a veneer of caring. How? That's a core focus of this book—and what's been missing from the conversation about authentic leadership.

The solution came to us as a light-bulb moment after reading the actual definition of the word *authentic*. All it means is being true to yourself. That's terrifying! You could be the biggest asshole on the planet and still be a textbook authentic leader, just because you're true to yourself. We realized that being an authentic leader is not enough. So, we developed the concept of Invested Leadership to take authentic leadership to the next level.

The path is simple. First, develop and cultivate self-awareness, via a collection of strategies we will outline, with the goal of identifying your interpersonal strengths and weaknesses, as well as those of others on your leadership team. Next, investigate *how* your employees actually need to be cared for. Then, fill those needs in two ways:

execute what you can on your own while filling in the gaps by partnering with others on your leadership team who have different caring skillsets than you do.

Think about this last idea as if we are talking about any standard C-suite. CEOs don't typically handle, for example, marketing and accounting. They hire a CMO and CFO. They rely on a variety of specialized professionals to run a successful business. Similarly, as the leader of a team or organization, you'll need others on the team to buttress your interpersonal weaknesses or amplify your strengths; this strategy is paramount.

The authentic-leadership revolution has seemingly led a slew of individual leaders to try to be everything to everyone. Instead, embrace Invested Leadership. Employees will get the care they need and deserve, without inauthenticity coming down from the top. You'll develop trust and be rewarded with loyalty, not to mention an increase in productivity and employee retention. Improvements will also be sustainable, and the process will protect you from the damaging effects of an echo chamber and the corrupting nature of power. Invested Leadership will ensure that you continue to be an effective, inspiring, and successful leader.

Honestly, ensuring that your employees receive care and empathy—either by you or someone else—should be as important to a CEO as are marketing or accounting. If you fail at that, culture will quickly turn toxic and you'll fail as a leader, no matter what leadership style you adopt.

WHO WE ARE (INCLUDING YOU)

If you're reading this book, you likely already understand that good leaders are always learning. Those who fancy themselves leaders but don't think they have room to grow have already failed, but that's not you. You know that, even though it sounds cliché as hell, leadership is a journey. So, you're always looking for a fresh take on an old topic. Maybe you have a company struggling with morale or retention. Or maybe you work at one of those companies and realize you have leadership skills going unused. Maybe you realize that people follow you even though leadership isn't in your job description and want to learn how to be part of a larger leadership team.

EVERY GREAT LEADER IS A STUDENT OF LEADERSHIP.

Either way, you recognize that leadership is a skill, not a natural inborn talent. Some people have incredible charisma that others are drawn to—where the term *born leader* comes from—but that, in and of itself, is not leadership. That's no different than a force of magnetism that creates a cult of personality. Attracting people to you is not necessarily leadership; in fact, at one point in time, it was even thought that introverts are somehow less effective as leaders than extroverts, which is not true.

Rather, every great leader is a student of leadership. World-class leaders understand it is a skill requiring constant practice. One doesn't just decide, *I'm a leader, and I'm done.* The moment you think that, by definition, you are not a leader, because leaders constantly strive to improve themselves and others. Development as a leader happens in that order: you improve yourself, and then you can improve others. If you're simply replicating other leaders without improving yourself, you're not improving others as much as you could be.

If you're reading this book, you are likely ready to do the work; you're ready to be introspective and honest with yourself. Invested Leadership requires taking a true accounting of your skillsets and deficits (to actually listen to feedback!), and then fill any potholes, whether through your own efforts or via partnership. This book can also help those who feel unable to execute actual caring themselves. Many leaders feel overwhelmed by the authentic-leadership revolution, whether they are introverted, narcissistic, or otherwise (we actually believe this book is the antidote to the ill effects of narcissism; more on that in Chapter 1). We are offering a path that helps them recognize they don't have to force it. They can surround themselves with people who genuinely have the necessary skillsets.

The two of us are also driving constantly to improve our leadership skills. That's ultimately how we ended up writing this book. The Invested Leadership concept developed out of lessons learned over our combined career paths, especially the almost two decades we spent as colleagues. There, we came to appreciate one another's dedication to growth, employees, the growth of employees, and leadership more generally. At Maestro, our clients typically hire us to help them streamline operations, scale their organizations, or implement new legal technologies. No matter what they hire us for, our clients consistently find, once we're in the door, that our real value is in leadership work—because, almost always, the client's biggest problem is one of leadership and culture. The variety and depth (and success) of our collective experiences gives us a pulpit from which to communicate what we see the industry doing wrong.

If our clients are overly focused on operations and underfocused on people, they suffer, especially if they are in the business of offering professional services: people are their product. When we walk into a new company, we always lead with discussions of culture, and winning hearts and minds. For example, we talk about earning the right to be heard. Sometimes, principals and CEOs think they've earned the right to be heard by virtue of their position. That's not true at all. In reality, you earn that right by walking into the office and asking people how they're doing, genuinely caring about the responses, and being present with them during the conversation. You earn that right by helping somebody out when you see they're stressed, or by redirecting them toward an area in which they can succeed and then coaching them up. Otherwise, the way you'll be "heard" is as a child hears a scolding parent—and the response you'll receive in turn will be just as perfunctory.

Our clients rarely recognize when they are the architects of their own misery; nobody says, "I have a leadership problem." They might cop to having a culture problem but admitting to a quote-unquote leadership problem is often too personal. Nevertheless, the system changes we implement often include processes designed to complement and buttress that leader's style, strength, and weaknesses. They hire us to fix their people; in reality, we often fix how they engage with their people.

We eventually began thinking of and discussing ways to contribute even more to the cause of developing emotional intelligence in the workplace. When we started writing this book, it was on the role of emotional intelligence in leadership, specifically focusing on authentic leadership. It was during that research when we realized that authentic leadership, without a focus on being a caring leader, can be a dangerous idea.

In our experience with professional-services organizations, however, we increasingly saw that people in leadership were thinking, *If this is how I feel, then that is good; that's authentic leadership.* When authenticity is self-focused instead of people-focused, then one could be true to oneself and also be destructively toxic. In practice, authentic leadership has assumed that leaders will authentically care about people. That is not what we've seen. Much of what's written and thought about authentic leadership fails to make such a distinction.

For decades, we had thought authentic leadership was the greatest style; then we realized it could also be the most toxic. We still think the key to leadership is emotional intelligence, that your ability to harness that is directly proportional to your ability to lead people. We've just taken that concept a step beyond authentic leadership to develop the theory of Invested Leadership.

Ultimately, writing the book is an extension of our own roles as leaders, in that we want to pass on and teach others how to be good leaders. We've been doing it in our personal lives and in our business lives. Now, this book is an opportunity to expand that mission into the larger world, to build even more great leaders by sharing what we've learned so far.

STACIE'S MOTIVATION

My leadership journey began by witnessing the profound impacts—both positive and negative—that leaders have on others. I was inspired by those who led with excellence and driven to do better by those who fell short. I internalized those lessons, cultivating the strengths I admired and rejecting the weaknesses I observed. Now, I'm passionate about sharing my experience, empowering others to become the kind of leaders who inspire action and create positive change.

ERIC'S MOTIVATION

"Whenever two Marines are together, one of them is in charge." These words, etched in my memory from Marine Corps boot camp, redefined leadership for me. I learned that leadership meant prioritizing the welfare of those in my charge. It meant ensuring their needs were met before my own. This early lesson instilled in me the power of selfless service and the importance of genuine care in building trust and inspiring action. True leadership isn't about titles; it's about putting others first.

WHERE WE'RE GOING TOGETHER

This book highlights the path toward Invested Leadership. Let's start with a couple of significant disclaimers. First, this is a journey, not a destination; we certainly don't mean to claim that we have "arrived." We are works in progress, as all leaders should be. The very best leaders are constantly learning and evolving. Further, we aren't suggesting the leaders we highlight in case studies have "gotten there" either (in fact, some of them are problematic in a variety of ways, which we will discuss). We only mean to highlight important behaviors we know to be effective means of displaying healthy, strong leadership, and share pathways toward the adoption of those behaviors.

Second, although the principles of Invested Leadership are as old as time (now you know why we opened the book with a discussion of *The Art of War*), the path to approach it is new. Honestly, in some ways, our argument is just common sense. If you're growing a plant, but decide not to water it, fertilize it, place it in sun, or show it attention, why would you reasonably expect it to flourish? If you have someone who's invaluable to you in the workplace, how is it not good business to meet their needs as a human, which is irreducible from their identity as an employee? People bring their whole selves to work—and you want them to, or they wouldn't perform very well.

This tried-and-true concept simply got lost somewhere in modern corporate America. Companies used to exercise a lot more care for their employees, but as information has become more commoditized in society, corporations lean more and more on data. To be clear, we are data people; organizations live and die by gleaning and responding to information, but using data to make decisions doesn't mean ignoring people. That's the mistake businesses have made. As they became more data driven, they started viewing people as costs. Employees became part of the bottom line and no longer humans, just expenses.

That's not always the case, of course. For example, we know of a law firm that is overstaffed (in our opinion, especially with our inclination to optimize operations). The firm refuses to let anyone go because they consider their people "family." The firm wants to increase revenue so it can keep the staff gainfully employed—not just increase profit for the principal. That's powerful. Sadly, it's also anachronistic, hearkening to a time when businesses felt more responsibility for the welfare of their communities.

Regardless, caring for people isn't typically such an expensive undertaking (we don't recommend overstaffing). When you consider the incredible return on investment from care—people who are more efficient and productive, and a more profitable company—it seems insane that one wouldn't make the simple basic effort to exercise care. A Gallup poll determined the biggest predictor of whether someone stays in a job is whether or not they have a best friend at work.[5] That's not because they want someone to hang out with; rather it's because they want to know that someone in the organization actually gives a shit about them. If there are people at your office who feel that no one truly cares about them, they will leave. You'll lose more money by not being Invested—after all, replacing an employee, by some estimates, costs about two times that employee's annual salary.[6]

There are two major ways to make a company more profitable: decrease costs or increase revenue. If you make your existing workforce more efficient, you'll see revenue increase. Many instead think myopically about the easiest way to get profitable fast, and they cut expenses, including people. Come in, chop expenses, increase efficiency and revenue, and then flip that company. That's the playbook. Businesses like this are looking for an easy way out, the quickest way to profit, instead of investing in their people, which ultimately leads to the most profit. (For what it's

---

5   Alok Patel and Stephanie Plowman, "The Increasing Importance of a Best Friend at Work," Gallup, August 17, 2022, updated January 19, 2024, https://www.gallup.com/workplace/397058/increasing-importance-best-friend-work.aspx.

6   Shane McFeely and Ben Wigert, "This Fixable Problem Costs U.S. Businesses $1 Trillion," Gallup, March 13, 2019, https://www.gallup.com/workplace/247391/fixable-problem-costs-businesses-trillion.aspx.

worth, we've never been hired to come in and fire people; we don't believe in it, as a matter of philosophy, because cutting your way to profitability is not sustainable.)

The Jack Welch revolution, led by his book *Winning*, suggested that cutting 10 percent of your workforce annually keeps a company lean and profitable. Setting aside those who get laid off, let's consider the remaining 90 percent— how did they feel when the others got whacked? That 90 percent was now in the running to be next year's 10 percent. We don't believe *Winning* tackled that effectively. Such a tactic may streamline productivity in the short term, but it creates a culture of extreme competition, fear, and low morale. Sun Tzu didn't advise decimating your own army on the regular. If you can, instead, increase revenue by investing in your people, by viewing them as humans instead of disposable parts, assuming business fundamentals are in line, profits are limitless in theory. We believe that if all externalities are equal, a caring enterprise is very likely to make more money than an uncaring enterprise.

People typically don't think of soft skills as money-making skills; that's finally changing, thank goodness. Even once leaders have buy-in, though, they don't always know how to develop those skills, cultivate and identify them in others, and execute them companywide. Besides, the truth is that sometimes they can't develop the skills, and, again, that's okay. Invested Leadership accounts for such a lack, recognizes that disingenuous efforts at soft skills are counterproductive, and offers another solution. With that in mind, here's a brief breakdown of what you'll learn in the following pages.

- In Chapters 1 and 2, we will explore the most common leadership styles, whether traditional or modern, in order to understand why they leave much to be desired. We will pay particular attention to the inadequacies of authentic leadership, the dangers of narcissism, and why Invested Leadership is the antidote to toxic authority.
- Then, in Chapters 3 through 5, we will get our hands dirty and take inventory—three inventories, to be exact. We will discuss why you must cultivate awareness of your strengths and weaknesses, as well as how to actually do it. Next, we'll do the same for those on your leadership team, as well as any "Queen Bees" on your staff (those who have the hearts and minds of your employees, whether they have formal titles or not, and control a lot more than you may realize). Then, you'll take an inventory of your employees' needs, of what they want out of their workplace experience, and how they actually want to be cared for.
- Finally, we will turn toward the implementation of the data you just gathered. We'll work through how to build trust and engender loyalty by ensuring your employees are genuinely cared for.
- Along the way, at the beginning of each chapter, we've included some of our favorite quotes regarding the content explored. We love quotes; we find them particularly helpful in this endeavor because they illustrate that, even if Invested Leadership is new, the ideas supporting it are not. The principles are time honored. You don't have to take our word for it.

The dirty secret in business leadership is that most people think caring in the workplace is bullshit. We can't tell you how many times we've heard the phrase *touchy-feely* in response to discussions of any soft skills. Empathy has become feminized by some alpha males. Now you know the other reason why we're opening with a quote *The Art of War*. Here it is again: "Regard your soldiers as your children, and they will follow you into the deepest valleys; look upon them as your own beloved sons, and they will stand by you even unto death."

Silly macho blowback to workplace caring—which, let's be honest, is really just fear—is also why we tell so many stories about the US Marines, an organization defined by caring. Emotional intelligence knows no gender. As Nobel Prize–winning physicist Donna Strickland once said, "I don't think women are more caring than men. That's just as offensive as saying women aren't as smart as men."[7]

We're not talking about being a good or bad person. We're talking about being an effective or ineffective leader. What's important is the self-awareness to recognize your blind spots, own them, and find ways to fill them in, either through your own growth or with the skillsets of others on your leadership team. That's what this book will help you do.

Invested Leadership is transformative. You transform yourself. You transform your leadership structure by partnering. You transform your employees by making them feel whole, appreciated, and loyal. And you may well transform your organization into a leaner and more profitable and productive entity—simply because people trust you and know you care. The sky is the limit.

---

7   Brian Keating, Focus Like a Nobel Prize Winner (Lioncrest, 2025).

"People don't care how much you know until they know how much you care."

—JOHN C. MAXWELL

"To win in the marketplace, you must first win in the workplace."

—DOUG CONANT

"Too often we underestimate the power of a touch, a smile, a kind word, a listening ear, an honest compliment, or the smallest act of caring, all of which have the potential to turn a life around."

—LEO BUSCAGLIA

"Love and compassion are necessities, not luxuries. Without them humanity cannot survive."

—DALAI LAMA

"No one has ever become poor by giving."

—ANNE FRANK

"Caring about others, running the risk of feeling, and leaving an impact on people, brings happiness."

—HAROLD KUSHNER

"People will forget what you said, people will forget what you did, but people will never forget how you made them feel."

—CARL W. BUEHNER

CHAPTER 1

WHAT GOT US HERE WON'T GET US THERE

"The greatest danger in times of turbulence is not the turbulence; it is to act with yesterday's logic."

—PETER DRUCKER

Steve Jobs's first stint with Apple was very different than his second one. Something shifted just enough that, post exit and reentry, he was able to take the company from struggling to world dominating.

The man always had brilliance and vision, but there is not a biography or documentary about him that paints a flattering picture of Jobs as a human. That personality type was part of his downfall: he eventually got sideways with his board, which terminated him. Later, when the board decided to bring him back, despite his flaws, because he really was the company's product guy, something had changed in Jobs. He recognized he needed to adjust some of his detrimental behaviors. He softened his approach. The second time around, he was still an autocratic, paternalistic, and narcissistic leader (in our opinion, and we will discuss those terms later in this chapter), but even within those structures and styles, he had become much more self-aware.

There's very little comparison to how successful (by almost every business metric) Apple was during his second round of leadership versus his first. They were a dying company at the end of his first tenure. During his second, they took off and now dominate not only the market but, in many ways, American culture.

It's not that he suddenly had better ideas. The company's meteoric success was due to a different kind of change in Jobs. He recognized he needed to be a different kind of leader. The second time around, he realized he needed people. In turn, that gave him a better understanding of what people needed from him.

THE PATH BEHIND US

Leadership is not an academic exercise. You can get an MBA in management, but managing isn't the same as leading. As the late business scholar Warren Bennis argued in his seminal book *On Becoming a Leader*, managers focus on systems and structures while leaders focus on people. When systems and people get conflated, it's very easy for the former to overtake the latter. The most effective organizations understand the importance of both, as separate pieces of a high-functioning enterprise. Organizations that treat their people like machinery get the same in response: a transactional, transient, uninspired workforce that makes no long-term commitment.

For that matter, not every principal or CEO is necessarily a leader. Sometimes, the guy slinging boxes in the warehouse has a firmer grasp on employees' hearts and minds—because he actually cares about his fellow workers. Leaders exist throughout any organization, whether in management or not. We don't believe you need some special training to be a leader. Working with and caring about people are the only skills necessary.

That said, leaders are constantly learning and growing, consuming theories and attending conferences. Countless books and videos have been published on the topic of leadership, including, of course, the one in your hands. Before we move forward, let's look at where we've been. We will later explain in more depth what Invested Leadership is, how to achieve and practice it, and why it's the future. First, let's investigate the major structures and styles of the past—and why they leave so much to be desired.

COMMON STRUCTURES AND STYLES

Everyone is, to some degree, whether intentionally or not, a leader. If you accept that to be true, and we do, then everyone necessarily fits into certain leadership structures and exhibits certain leadership styles. There are a million resources out there defining classic leadership structures and styles; we don't need to be the million and first, so we chose to discuss only four of each and will do so with brevity.

STRUCTURES
Autocratic:

Dictatorial. My way or the highway. I am the decider in chief. The buck stops here.

Pros: Autocratic structures are efficient, the quickest ways to get from point A to point B. Employees know where to go to get answers. Autocrats can determine pretty quickly whether or not their decisions work.

Cons: An autocratic structure is not always enjoyable and positive for employees. They often feel unheard, as if their opinions don't matter—or only matter if they agree with the autocrat's opinions.

It's common for autocrats to be perceived as assholes. That is not always the case, of course. However, it is true that autocrats are often narcissists. When this structure is paired with a narcissistic style, workplace culture can be very toxic. To be clear, the problem is not the autocracy; the problem is the narcissism. Autocrats probably have the greatest need to buttress their structures with an Invested Leadership team comprised of people who can fill in their blind spots in order to meet employees' needs.

Democratic:

Go around the room and build consensus. Consensus carries the day.

Pros: Everyone feels heard. And feels ownership in the decision.

Cons: Often, groupthink is not the best way to make a decision. Say a group plans to vote on which stock to invest in. One person might have expertise in a certain area with hot stocks that no one else has heard of. Instead, the masses vote for a vanilla, low-growth, standby stock and no one makes any money.

People with a Machiavellian style take advantage of democratic structures by manipulating participants in order to guide decisions. Again, the problem is not the structure but the style.

Paternalistic:

Old school. Personality driven. There's someone who's been in the business forever and you think of them as the grandfather of sorts. Maybe it's a family business with a patriarch or matriarch at the top of the brand, or a strong founder-based business that acts on the vision of that founder. It is very close to autocracy, except with more deference than control; power is given, rather than taken, by the person at the top.

Pros: There's an innate respect for the founder or person at the top. Typically, success has been achieved by the person at the top, so the company sticks with what works.

Cons: The structure makes it pretty easy to take advantage of people. The person at the top might feel they can ask more of family members, or perhaps employees have fallen for a cult of personality and are vulnerable to exploitation. WeWork would be a failed paternalistic model. Further, this is not a scalable structure: typically, when the person at the top dies, so goes the engine and the rudder.

Laissez-Faire:

Hands off. I provide support and mentoring when needed, but otherwise offer little guidance, instead delegating to team members.

Pros: Minimal micromanagement. Employees feel empowered and take more ownership. Innovation and problem-solving flow.

Cons: Employees can lack direction. Some may require more guidance. If employees or teams are not communicating, they might duplicate work or waste time on disadvantageous pursuits.

STYLES
Narcissistic:

Charismatic leadership. The spotlight is on me, what I want for the business, and how I can be personally elevated. I'm the most important person in the room so you need me. I want you to like me.

Pros: They make great salespeople and can generate a lot of revenue. They're very good at influencing and swaying opinion.

Cons: Sometimes they don't care about anybody besides themselves, which creates a dangerously toxic culture.

Machiavellian:

When someone has a high EQ—and uses it to manipulate people toward their goals. They know how to play people.

Pros: Someone who can see and play out long-game strategy is clutch in any business.

Cons: Employees and clients can feel played or manipulated, leading the strategy to backfire.

Authentic:

One of the foremost thinkers on the topic of authentic leadership writes, "Authenticity is the alignment of the head, mouth, heart, and feet—thinking, saying, feeling, and doing the same thing—consistently. This builds trust, and followers love leaders they can trust."[8] That's true in theory. But such an alignment doesn't necessarily lead to trust unless the foundation of the head, mouth, and heart is one defined by caring about others in the organization.

Pros: Positive authentic leadership that inspires people can create trust and engagement, which is associated with greater job satisfaction, communication, and a stronger sense of purpose for individuals. Organizations benefit from increased productivity and a positive work environment.

Cons: When a person with antisocial tendencies or who lacks empathy is told to be nothing but true to themselves, without having someone else on the team to exhibit emotional intelligence, a dangerously toxic work culture develops.

Invested:

You know yourself. You know your people. You can either adapt to your people or bring others around you who can, and you're never done growing and learning.

Pros: That's where we're headed.

Cons: We literally can't think of any.

INVEST IN EACH

We've been students of leadership for a long time. Many theories present structures as distinct and unchanging.

---

8   Lance Secretan, The Spark, the Flame, and the Torch: Inspire Self. Inspire Others. Inspire the World (The Secretan Center, 2010).

Adam is a laissez-faire leader. Catherine is a maternalistic leader. As though leaders are one-trick ponies. That has not been our experience. Your business can dictate which structure works best for you, and it may be necessary to pivot structures at any given time. Sophisticated leaders won't be pigeonholed in any one structure. Rather, they see them as tools they can pull from their toolbox as needed.

Think of structures like vehicles. The driver is the style. If I'm going to meet a client, I would drive my BMW there. If I'm going to help a friend move, I would drive my pickup truck. Depending on your business decision, you'll need to employ different structures at different times.

Additionally, no structure is better than another. Eric was on a panel once and referenced the principal of the firm as an autocratic leader. Then, another member of the panel (nicely) chastised Eric because he understood the use of the phrase as a pejorative rather than a descriptive. He thought Eric was calling the autocrat a jerk. Rather, Eric was simply describing the decision-making process the principal typically employs. No structure in and of itself is toxic. But any structure can become toxic, depending on the style injected into it.

Invested Leadership, as a style, pairs successfully with any structure. For example, you could practice an Invested style within an autocratic structure. In that case, the leader cares about people, seeks their feedback, and makes decisions with their interests in mind—but nevertheless executes unilateral decisions. Alternatively, an Invested Leader within a democratic structure might procure everyone's feedback and let the best idea win following a free give-and-take. The tech world vibes much more with the latter while smaller businesses are typically more autocratic.

We're not telling you what structure to use. We're here to proselytize about style—specifically, the Invested style.

Granted, most leaders employ several styles throughout their tenures. We both have exhibited elements of Machiavellianism. That in and of itself doesn't disqualify one from a position of leadership (or make one a bad person). The point is also to have elements of the Invested style and to lean into those more and more, as they will give you the self-awareness and recognition needed to meet both employee needs and business needs simultaneously. Regardless of the structure in which you operate at any given moment, or the different style elements that compose your leadership profile, you need to care about people authentically and/or have a leadership team around you that does.

THE ANTIDOTE TO TOXICITY

Dare we say that many historic leaders and top business leaders exhibit at least some degree of narcissism. That doesn't have to be a bad thing! The challenge comes when a leader fails to acknowledge this and seeks other ways to give employees what they need. Narcissistic behavior—forcing everyone to bend to your will and needs—doesn't lead to trust. It simply can't. Therefore, it will also diminish optimal performance and retention. Employees require meaningful purpose. They often get that from their leader. Show us a toxic culture; we'll show you a toxic leader.

If you take and take, and give nothing in return, you'll see their backsides as they walk away—no matter how quote-unquote authentic you are. Unless you round out your approach to employees, you will drive talent away.

Authenticity is not necessarily the answer. Care is what

builds trust, not authenticity alone. There's an assumption undergirding the idea of authentic leadership that being one's authentic self also means being one's best self, but this assumption doesn't always bear out in practice, especially among narcissists, who already believe they are their best selves. We have seen several business leaders who flat-out admit to being narcissists. They even use it as an explanation for why they can't perceive the experiences of others in their organization. While we applaud their candor, we find it problematic that they think announcing it will solve any potential problems created by this leadership style. If they consider themselves to be authentic leaders, they may feel that, for the most part, their leadership work is done.

Another example: Donald Trump is a textbook authentic leader. Whether you like him or not, you can't deny that he's 100 percent himself. Similarly, both his critics and fans describe him as wily and often not to be trusted. Authenticity does not equal trustworthiness. The whole concept of authentic leadership has been functioning under the assumption that a leader's behavior is positive for employees, but that's not always the case. We believe that the entire hypothesis behind classically defined authentic leadership is fundamentally flawed.

One of the problems with authentic leadership is that people think it's enough simply to say, "This is me; I'm giving you who I am and therefore I'm an authentic leader." We are suggesting that, for some, authenticity isn't enough. Authentic them isn't what employees need. As a basic foundation, you really have to ask yourself, *Do I really care about this person?* If the answer is no, then...well, you need to keep reading this book.

Consider the story of an office manager at the law firm of

one of our clients. Let's call her Lana. She was working hard to inspire her subordinates and others who were junior to her. As a result, many among the staff were drawn to Lana, and saw her as a natural leader. Their boss was toxic—which also contributed to people turning toward her, since they couldn't turn toward him. So Lana was also working overtime to counteract the effects of his behavior and policies.

He crossed the line with her when he began "coaching" her to be inauthentic with the staff. Specifically, there was an employee on staff who was very valuable to the boss but was also a toxic presence in the organization. Let's call the employee Henry. Lana could see he was dangerous and was damaging other people and the culture at large. When she took this to the boss, the boss asked Lana to create a fictionalized relationship with Henry, so everyone else on staff would respect him more and believe the operation was unencumbered by drama. It was a farce because the operation was obviously not running smoothly.

Lana argued that Henry was actually not delivering value because of his toxic effects, but the boss seemingly had his head in the sand. Lana refused to pretend she had a close and effective working relationship with Henry. It ran counter to her character. Eventually, she gave her notice. This boss lost the most effective leader he had on his team. Choosing inauthenticity in service of the bottom line is completely antithetical to the concepts of Invested Leadership.

Plenty of leaders out there are narcissistic to some degree yet recognize the increasing need for a positive culture when it comes to retaining talent. Invested Leadership is the antidote to toxic culture and to narcissism's ill effects. By practicing what we preach, you can either develop your own ways of caring for employees or find someone else on your team who could fill those needs for you (which is a way of acknowledging those needs and ensuring they are met). Otherwise, those who can't see people as anything but widgets may want to reconsider whether or not they are actually leaders—their "followers" will have already determined they are not leaders.

If the boss sitting at top does not display leadership, then the boss needs to have a team who can. We argue Invested Leadership is the highest form of leadership. Let's say a boss is totally transactional and wants to get the most juice out of the employee squeeze, but the boss doesn't genuinely care about employees. Further, the employees recognize that the boss is a jerk. Via the Invested Leadership model, a leadership team sits between the boss and the employees, filling in the boss's blind spots and caring for employees. Meanwhile, the narcissist is free to go execute whatever their superpower may be without losing productivity or talent because of their inability to care for employees or, worse, because they pretend to care for employees (a practice that always backfires).

A charismatic, me-driven, paternalistic leader can only succeed until an organization scales because, at that point, more people are necessarily needed to lead the organization...but the aforementioned leadership style cannot be scaled. That's the beautiful thing about Invested Leadership: if done the right way, even narcissists can have a positive, healthy, leadership ecosystem by bringing onto their leadership teams people who will legitimately and authentically deliver caring.

Caring is the solution, not authenticity alone. When you genuinely care or bring people onto the leadership team who can, you will see all of your people excel—even, and maybe especially, those who had struggled under prior "management" styles. You will also see the next generation of leaders evolving, as they are naturally drawn to the Invested style and want it for themselves.

KEY TAKEAWAYS

- Leadership structures, such as autocratic, democratic, paternalistic, and laissez-faire, are in the toolbox of any great leader, who chooses a structure depending on a project's needs.
- Leadership styles are less fungible and more likely to affect employee retention. The most involved and effective leadership style is Invested.
- Authenticity in leadership is a promising idea, and a buzzworthy term, but it is not enough, particularly among the vast majority of leaders exhibiting narcissistic styles.
- Invested Leadership is the antidote to narcissism.

"If you always do what you've always done, you'll always get what you've always gotten."

—ANONYMOUS

"Change is the law of life. And those who look only to the past or present are certain to miss the future."

—JOHN F. KENNEDY

"If you don't like something, change it. If you can't change it, change your attitude."

—MAYA ANGELOU

"The measure of intelligence is the ability to change."

—ALBERT EINSTEIN

"It is a great advantage to have many honest [people] near you, because it obliges you to be honest yourself."

—DUC DE LÉVIS

"We cannot solve our problems with the same thinking we used when we created them."

—ANONYMOUS

CHAPTER 2

EAT LAST

"Trust is the coin of the realm."

—GENERAL JAMES MATTIS, USMC

At every military base, at any given time, there is an "officer of the day," who is responsible for overseeing the daily operations and security of a military installation or unit for a twenty-four-hour period. The officer of the day is in charge of all personnel guarding the gate and is there in case something goes wrong. Typically, this post is populated by a low-level officer, such as a lieutenant, someone who is possibly even younger than those in their charge. One Christmas day, then-Brigadier General James Mattis (he would later go on to become a four-star Marine Corps general and United States Secretary of Defense) decided to serve this duty so the junior officer could be home with his family. This is not something generals typically do.

Meanwhile, General Charles Krulak, then-Commandant of the Marine Corps, and his wife had a tradition of delivering cookies to the Marines serving guard duty on Christmas.

So, on that Christmas Day, the commandant showed up, asking, "Who's the officer of the day?"

"Sir, it's Brigadier General Mattis," replied the lance corporal who was on duty.

General Krulak said, "No, no, no. I know who General Mattis is. I mean, who's the officer of the day today, Christmas Day?"

The lance corporal, now anxious, replied, "Sir, it is Brigadier General Mattis."

Spotting a cot in the back room, Krulak said, "No, Lance Corporal. Who slept in that bed last night?"

"Sir, it was Brigadier General Mattis."

Then, here came Mattis in a duty uniform, carrying a sword. Krulak said, "Jim, what are you doing here on Christmas Day? Why do you have duty?"[9] General Mattis explained that he had chosen to serve the duty in place of the young officer because the latter had a family. Mattis wanted the young officer to spend Christmas with his family.

Mattis had nothing to gain personally from making such a choice. He did it solely to brighten the day of one Marine and, as a result, inspire everyone else on duty. His whole career, he was known for moves like this. Mattis is an erudite history buff and lifelong student of leadership, but don't misunderstand: he is also your stereotypical hard-ass Marine. His nickname was "Mad Dog" after all. During his career, he wasn't someone you wanted to mess around with, and his Marines loved him.

Mattis distills his leadership fundamentals into what he calls the three Cs: competence, caring, and conviction.

---

9   "A General Mattis Christmas Story," U.S. Naval Institute Blog, December 2010, https://blog.usni.org/posts/2010/12/17/a-general-mattis-christmas-story.

Competence is being brilliant in the basics; you don't have to be in Mensa, but you must know the basics. Second, he had a way of saying that nobody cares how much you know until they know how much you care. Finally, he believed in understanding and conveying conviction, what you will and won't stand for. There are many more illustrations of his dedication to these tenets. For example, he sometimes joined his Marines on the front lines during combat; again, generals generally don't usually do this. Little inspires Marines more than having their officers in the trenches with them.

General Mattis talked about recruiting for attitude and then training up for skill. In other words, character is what matters. He wanted Marines who would take bullets for one another and have the capacity to develop trusting and caring relationships. The rest can be taught. As a leader, Mattis recognized the whole person in his subordinates. He wrote and spoke often about "trust as the coin of the realm." If people know who you are, what you're about, and that you care for them, that necessarily builds trust. Once you have trust, you have everything. You could say, "Hey, we're going to take this hill," and even if they think that's a crazy idea, they'll trust that you know something they don't or have already thought through the strategic initiatives and casualties.

Mattis's caring attitude is indicative of the US Marines in general. Eric served as a Marine, so we are partial, but still: The organization as a whole is one that promotes doing for others before doing for oneself. When you are in charge—and whenever two or more Marines are together, someone is in charge—you do not eat, drink, sleep, or even sit down, until you have personally seen that everyone else in your charge has done the same. When you're in charge, as a Marine, you are endowed with a sacred trust to care for those in your charge—so it is with Invested Leadership.

> INVESTED LEADERS STAND BENEATH ALL OF THE PEOPLE THEY ARE RESPONSIBLE FOR AND ASK, "WHAT DO THEY NEED AND HOW CAN I GIVE IT TO THEM?"

INVERT THE PYRAMID

Because of the popularity of authentic leadership, it's been possible for some leaders to think all they need to be is true to themselves, and therefore they are authentic. It's possible to assume that, if they are at the top of the pyramid, they are leaders. We want to flip that pyramid upside down. Invested Leaders stand beneath all of the people they are responsible for and ask, "What do they need and how can I give it to them?"

An Invested Leader understands that caring for people is ultimately what makes an organization succeed. No initiatives, rollouts, or organization change will be effective if the employees responsible for implementing them don't feel genuinely cared for. Now that more people work from home, people have more choices in the market, and there is greater diversity of workspaces, leaders have an even greater need to connect with people.

To be clear, when we speak about caring, we mean interpersonal as well as physical needs. We're talking about the basic needs that, when met, make employees' lives better. This is not the same thing as having a bleeding heart or, for example, never firing anyone; nothing could be further from the truth. For that matter, caring for people is not the same thing as being selfless. We have been known to buy groceries for a paralegal, who also happened to be a single mom, because we knew she was struggling financially. That's not a selfless act; we didn't give her our groceries and therefore go without.

One need not be selfless in order to show care. Invested Leadership inspires people and drives them to do their best, in part because they don't want to let down the leadership team since that team hasn't let them down either. Maybe they thought they'd signed up for a nine-to-five job but then became inspired to the degree that they no longer even think of it as a job. Now they have vision and are imagining all they could be. Practicing Invested Leadership is like fertilizing and watering the employees in your organization—not so you can yank them out to consume them, but because you're growing an ecosystem.

We get satisfaction out of seeing people grow. If that benefits us or our teams, great, but the drive is to help people grow and encourage them to invest in themselves. That's what gets us out of bed and makes us want to continue working to become better leaders. When you lead that way, you also model that form of leadership in your employees, who in turn invest in and care for the next generation, becoming Invested Leaders themselves and strengthening the ecosystem.

Again, artificial caring will have the opposite effect; you can't just read this book and pretend to care. Don't worry;

we will explore how to develop and work your "caring muscles" and how to lean on others in your organization whenever you can't exhibit the kind of caring required. First, let's explore some of the most effective leadership traits.

CLASSIC TRAITS OF EFFECTIVE LEADERS

Invested Leaders still exhibit the hallmarks of leaders you've always admired. In this section, we explore some of the classic traits of effective leaders—but in a new light. There's more nuance to these characteristics than traditional definitions allow. Let's look at each through a new lens: that of Invested Leadership.

INTEGRITY

In this context, integrity and honesty are closely related. It is doing the right thing at the right time for the right reason. Specifically, we're talking about engaging in self-evaluation to determine your flaws and buttress them, as well as to determine your strengths and amplify them. Ask yourself what you're good at and not good at, and, perhaps more important, whether or not you're willing to change. You should be willing to answer those questions before you do any work toward developing yourself as a leader.

COMMUNICATION

At its most basic form, communication is giving a message and then ensuring it was heard and understood. The most effective communication, though, is loving communication: candid, appropriate, sometimes tough, but always done in the other person's best interest. Loving communication is executed with the goal of making the person and the organization better. There are additional benefits to communicating this way: when your people understand this is your genuine, default position, they will be less likely to misread the tone of an email, for example, or allow miscommunications or misunderstandings. If those do occur, your people will feel safe enough to come to you with questions or concerns. This, of course, gives you opportunities to seek feedback, the kind of give-and-take that shows even more caring and develops even more trust.

WORK ETHIC

Work ethic is sometimes conflated with being a workaholic. Those are not the same thing. As Invested Leaders, we are not looking for our people to put in fifteen-hour days (we've both done that, and it is a path to burnout). Rather, we want to inspire people to give their absolute best during the number of hours they committed to work, which may differ from person to person. Maybe, for some, giving their best means going hard for fifty minutes of each hour and then taking ten-minute breaks to walk around so their minds can rest or recharge, allowing for creativity to bloom again. We would not judge work ethic solely based on how many widgets were produced but on the quality and integrity of a person's effort and investment. For that matter, Invested Leaders exemplify the same kind of integrity in their own work ethics. Everybody's got a story about a boss who just drinks coffee and points at all there is to be done. When your people hear you state a work goal, and then see you putting in the effort to achieve it, they will deliver the same kind of commitment in return.

A BOSS IS NOT NECESSARILY A LEADER.

ADAPTABILITY

This is one of the hallmarks of Invested Leadership. You won't at first know what your employees need and how to meet them where they're at. The process necessarily requires adaptability. People talk about the intrinsic need for a business to be adaptable; so must leadership be adaptable to the changing needs of a staff. Eric was once in a position to help a female employee escape a domestic-abuse situation. Certainly, this is typically the sort of crisis problem-solving that would fall to friends and family or social services, but because we were at a law firm, we were uniquely positioned to advocate that her abuser receive some amount of jail time, which gave her an opportunity to fully extricate herself.

RESPECT

A boss is not necessarily a leader. That bears restating: a boss is not necessarily a leader. The classic leadership model says the person in charge is the boss and should be respected. We think it should be the other way around: the Invested Leader should respect the people in their charge. Ultimately, that builds up respect for the leader in turn. In the workplace, you cannot truly respect a person if you don't totally respect the person. You may not approve of certain behaviors or decisions, but you still have to respect them as people. For example, in our experience, raising your voice to other employees will never engender respect. When people do what you say simply because you write their checks, that's not an example of respect but of fear or transaction. On the other hand, when you consistently demonstrate respect and care, and then ask your employees to take on something difficult, they will know it's important and commit their best efforts to getting the job done.

IT'S ABOUT FINDING THE CENTER OF THE VENN DIAGRAM BETWEEN CANDOR AND KINDNESS.

POSITIVITY

When a leader compliments someone's outfit and tells them to have a great day, that is a certain kind of positivity, but we're talking about behaving in ways that generate positive outcomes. For example, imagine responding to the first draft of a document you receive by saying, "This sucks; do it again." You probably won't get the most creative work out of that person, and if you do, you likely will have lost their respect. Instead, you might say, "I see where you were going with this. And I liked this part. But I think this other thought could be stronger if..." It's about finding the center of the Venn diagram between candor and kindness.

EMPATHY

There's a difference between intellectually understanding a circumstance and emotionally understanding it. The classic leadership response to an employee's house burning down is, "Geez, that's horrible. Can I donate to the cause to help get you back in your house?" However, that's not necessarily empathy. Empathy is understanding that this person lost their child's baby photos, which can't be replaced. Empathy is understanding that she may also need a hug, not only a check. She needs someone to understand the pain of what she's going through. Invested Leaders have an emotive approach to empathy rather than an intellectual one.

HUMOR

When you don't take yourself too seriously, you mitigate intimidation. Leaders can go a long way toward building trust by being a little effacing, which can reduce tension by humanizing them with humor. Perhaps this trait is unfair to include in the list, since not everyone naturally has a sense of humor. Regardless, in our experience, we have found humor to be an effective way to break through to people. That doesn't just mean dropping a "dad joke" every now and then, although there's nothing wrong with that (Eric insisted we include this sentence). The goal is to humanize yourself—with, for example, stories about your kid throwing spaghetti all over the kitchen floor or how often you break the copy machine—so those in your charge don't feel threatened by you, and can therefore develop more trust, respect, and loyalty.

KINDNESS AND APPRECIATION

This is about showing your humanity. Bringing someone else a coffee when you run to the store or buying somebody lunch are opportunities to show you're not rigid and stuffy, that you're a normal person. For that matter, a simple "thank you" goes miles and miles. In a traditional workplace relationship, where there's a boss and a worker, and the former pays the latter for a job, there's no need for thank-yous. As such, sharing authentic appreciation tells those in your charge that you are not engaging in a transactional relationship. Think of General Mattis sending that young officer home to his family for Christmas. Genuine acts of kindness are powerful, and Invested Leaders never pass opportunities to be kind because they understand the acts have power far beyond each moment. This is also, of course, strategic: when you need an employee to go above and beyond for some reason on some Friday afternoon, they'll be willing to because you've shown that you'd do it for them.

SELF-AWARENESS

Under the auspices of authentic leadership, being self-aware is simply knowing who you are. We take this concept a step further. By understanding your own limitations, you can better recognize how those limitations might affect the people you lead. This awareness empowers you to address those shortcomings and provide them with the fullest support possible. While authentic leadership encourages one to embrace "potholes," Invested Leadership asks one to identify those potholes and find ways to fill them in.

DETAIL ORIENTATION

You want to be able to focus on details not just in the work you do for the organization but also in the way you read others in the organization. Say someone in your charge arrives to the office looking haggard and you learn that he discovered the night prior that his child was diagnosed with cancer. No matter what fire needs to be extinguished at the office that day, you probably don't want to lean on him. Doing so could be detrimental to both him and the project. Find someone else to lean on until he's on steadier ground.

FAIRNESS

A leader's ability to assess situations and individuals objectively is essential for creating a fair and productive environment. While some team members may flourish under this direct style, leaders must be mindful of unconscious biases that can arise. Favoritism, even if unintentional, erodes trust and hinders team cohesion. Effective leaders prioritize self-awareness and actively work to create an inclusive environment where everyone feels supported and has the opportunity to succeed.

RESPONSIBILITY

Traditional leadership often focuses on organizational policies and procedures, such as adhering to time-off rules. Invested Leaders, however, recognize the importance of caring for the "whole person." Instead of simply following policy in the face of an employee's personal crisis, like losing a home to a fire, they seek ways to provide genuine support and understand that a return to 100 percent productivity may take time. Effectively, we are recommending to lead rather than rule.

COURAGE

Invested Leadership has to be willing to take risks for and on behalf of people. Sometimes that means tough conversations with otherwise high-performing people because they're creating conflicts that damage the group dynamic. Sometimes that means speaking up to someone above you in the chain of command because a new top-down edict will be unfair to those in your charge. Whatever the circumstance, when you've built up respect and trust, and exhibit integrity, you'll have enough capital to get through tough conversations.

Effectively, we are recommending to lead rather than rule. In some ways, this is simply restating the very basic idea of leading by example, of showing people the way rather than telling them where to go. Invested Leaders earn respect rather than demand it.

But what if you lack any of these classic traits of effective leadership? The authentic leader might simply accept the deficit and assume that they're a good-enough leader. Their thinking centers around the belief that what really matters is that they can do A, B, or C. Meanwhile, the Invested Leader will identify the interpersonal skills they lack, and either work to develop those skills or find others on the leadership team who do have the skills. Most classic CEOs recognize the need for a CFO who is strong in finance, a CMO who understands marketing, and others with specific business skills that round out those of the CEO. Invested Leadership simply treats interpersonal-leadership skills in the same way.

IF YOU'RE A LEADER, AND YOU DON'T HAVE A WHY, WE DOUBT YOU EVEN ARE A LEADER.

FIND YOUR "WHY"

We work with a lot of lawyers. Many of them entered the field without knowing their "Why." We believe this is why so many in the field are unhappy and don't recommend their careers to others. On the other hand, those lawyers who did have a "Why" before applying to schools? They think it's the greatest calling in the world. They are advocates for justice, policy, or whatever it is that lights them up and they're happy.

Ask yourself why you fundamentally want to be a leader—not an Invested Leader, but any leader at all. The best leaders we've met never answered, "Because I want to be a leader." If you jump into this process without understanding your motivation and deeper purpose behind the work, you're likely to fail. Frankly, if you're a leader, and you don't have a "Why," we doubt you are as effective a leader as you could be.

We don't mean to be accusatory. It's just that we see this all the time. You'd be surprised by how many people haven't thought much about their "Why." The problem? Vacuums want to be filled. When you can't articulate your "Why," something will inhabit that space, and it will usually be a desire for money or some other immediate personal concern, such as social status. These goals do not make a leader and cannot sustain the kind of leadership that leads to success.

We've even heard some say their "Why" is to get the corner office, a management position. But that is not the same thing as being a leader. In fact, such motivation signals they actually don't want to be a leader or at least don't understand what it is to be a leader. They might be charismatic and even successful, but those are not true leadership attributes. Of course, this person could one day develop an understanding of what leadership means, find their "Why," and then, perhaps get a corner office...but the office cannot be a "Why."

ERIC'S "WHY"

I'm drawn to the study of leadership because it's a path to continuous self-improvement. I believe in reaching my full potential and inspiring others to do the same. Witnessing that growth, both in myself and those around me, is incredibly rewarding.

STACIE'S "WHY"

I'm driven by a desire to share my knowledge and experience, to leave a lasting legacy by empowering the next generation of leaders. Nothing is more rewarding than witnessing someone I've mentored step into a leadership role and apply those lessons with their own unique perspective.

THINKING STRATEGICALLY

The transactional leader thinks, *I'm done being touchy-feely. It doesn't get me anywhere. There's no value in it. I just want to be transactional because everybody knows what the deal is: There's a job. I pay you for the job, and you get money for the job.* First of all, that means this leader is only as good as the next transactional relationship that comes along. By definition, they see no value in caring and develop no loyalty or connection. If it's really all "about the Benjamins," when someone else comes along, offering a bigger, better deal, that person will take it. Second, nearly every business goes through times of austerity. Trust and caring last longer than tough times do. People will give their leaders a tremendous benefit of the doubt during tough times if history has shown they can trust their leaders to take care of them. They will ride out austerity instead of leaving their leaders high and dry.

COMBINING EQ, IQ, AND EXPERIENCE EQUALS A SUPERPOWERED WORKPLACE.

This isn't just touchy-feely rhetoric. This is strategic thinking. Invested Leadership works toward the long-term good of the organization, its people, and its leaders. Invested Leadership develops people who will eventually become great leaders themselves, which in turn propels the organization forward. Such a style of leadership also encourages those in your charge to run through walls for you. Our purpose, of course, is not just to help you develop a workforce you can call on to drop everything at any given moment. Regardless, there will be times when that's needed of people—and if you've acknowledged boundaries, built trust, and earned respect, those in your charge will show up for you.

The benefits of Invested Leadership to a team and organization are nothing short of transformative. If you have a group of people who genuinely care about one another, we believe, all things being equal, you will be more successful than any competitor. It's very common to have a job that gives you a paycheck. It is less common to be part of a group of people not related to one another by biology, who genuinely care about each other. You see it sometimes in smaller organizations, such as startups, but rarely in larger organizations. We are hoping to spread the culture of genuine caring far and wide.

Emotional intelligence (or emotional quotient, EQ) is a necessity for Invested Leadership to thrive. That does not mean, however, that EQ is a necessary trait of an Invested Leader. What we demand is that the Invested Leader be aware of their EQ levels and buttress appropriately, either by consistently developing EQ, or bringing people around them who excel at it.

Historically, emotional intelligence—what we basically define as an awareness of yourself and others—has been viewed as a "soft skill." Traditionally, one was considered weak for exemplifying too many soft skills. Now, we recognize how stupid that is. In the 1950s and '60s, we used to think work happened at work and home life happened at home, but humans aren't wired that way. You don't turn off who you are just because you walk into an office. People want to be cared for in all settings. Combining EQ, IQ, and experience equals a superpowered workplace.

In the next chapters, we'll explore exactly how to achieve this.

KEY TAKEAWAYS

- Invert the pyramid: think about how you can serve those in your charge.
- The classic traits of effective leadership still apply, but you can take them a step further by viewing them through the lenses of service and caring.
- Determine your "Why" or else selfishness may determine it for you.
- When you have genuinely earned the trust and respect of those in your charge, your organization will be bulletproof.

"The first responsibility of a leader is to define reality. The last is to say thank you. In between, the leader is a servant."

—MAX DE PREE

"The true measure of a leader is not the number of people who serve him, but the number of people he serves."

—JOHN C. MAXWELL

"The growth and development of people is the highest calling of leadership."

—HARVEY S. FIRESTONE

"Leaders become great, not because of their power, but because of their ability to empower others."

—JOHN C. MAXWELL

"If your actions inspire others to dream more, learn more, do more, and become more, you are a leader."

—ANONYMOUS

"Leadership is about making others better as a result of your presence and making sure that impact lasts in your absence."

—SHERYL SANDBERG

"In the Marine Corps, we take care of each other. It's not just about the mission; it's about the Marines. You never leave a Marine behind."

—US MARINE CORPS SERGEANT MAJOR MICHEAL BARRETT

CHAPTER 3

HALL OF MIRRORS

"A true friend stabs you in the front."

—ANONYMOUS

Abraham Lincoln was an innovator, not least because he wanted the best and brightest in his cabinet. Not the best and brightest in his political party, but the best person in the country for each particular job, no matter their affiliation or agenda. He wanted to surround himself with ideas and talent, regardless of whether or not they agreed with him. He wasn't interested in sycophants. He wasn't afraid to be told he was wrong or have his practices or beliefs challenged. History has come to call this a "cabinet of rivals."

Lincoln's secretary of treasury, Salmon Chase, in particular, was even angling for the presidency, but he also had valuable political connections, which Lincoln needed. Chase, meanwhile, was a staunch abolitionist. Some historians believe it was Chase's advice that played a significant part in swaying Lincoln in that regard. Imagine if Chase hadn't had the freedom and invitation to have those conversations with President Lincoln?

Think of an organization as a plant. Surrounding it with only like-minded individuals creates an echo chamber, like a sealed jar. The perspectives within that jar become stagnant. Without the fresh air of diverse viewpoints and the nutrients of challenging ideas, the organization will wither and die. Change is essential for growth and survival.

Fast-forward 150 years from Lincoln's presidency, and Barack Obama did the same thing. Not only did he choose his primary opponent, Hillary Clinton, to be his secretary of state, he also had two Republicans in his cabinet: Robert Gates, secretary of defense, and Ray LaHood, secretary of transportation.

We are big believers in seeking perspectives outside of our own. We are each skewed and colored by our own experiences and biases. Those who challenge us offer invaluable perspectives that we might otherwise miss. Keeping these individuals close ensures not only better decision-making but also, as this chapter will reveal, cultivates a more well-rounded and effective leadership style. To achieve that, you need to create an environment where it's truly safe (and even encouraged) for people to give you feedback. It is important not only to respect those giving the feedback but also to seriously consider the feedback.

Anytime you have a conversation with someone who has the freedom to be honest with you, there is an opportunity to learn something about yourself, your team, and even the person speaking. Every opportunity to learn is a chance to grow, and embracing diverse perspectives is the key to unlocking that growth. Learning from those who challenge our thinking, and truly listening to and applying their feedback, can be transformative for our interpersonal skills and overall development. While surrounding ourselves with like-minded people may feel comfortable, it limits our exposure to new ideas and hinders our progress. A "cabinet of rivals," on the other hand, provides the intellectual friction and diverse viewpoints we need to sharpen our minds and reach our full potential.

PEOPLE WILL ACTUALLY IDENTIFY WITH AND RESPECT YOU MORE WHEN YOU RECOGNIZE YOUR WEAKNESSES.

KNOW YOURSELF FIRST

Invested Leadership is rooted in self-awareness: it requires more than just adopting certain traits; it demands authenticity. To lead effectively, you must first understand yourself. Without genuine self-awareness, your actions may appear forced or insincere, hindering your ability to connect with and inspire others. Take the time to honestly assess your strengths and weaknesses—this is the essential first step on your leadership journey. In our experience, many leaders are not accustomed to self-investigation and are not comfortable putting a microscope on themselves. There's pressure for leaders to have all the answers, which may lead them to feel that any admission of weakness or blind spots will make them lesser leaders. That misses the point. Everybody has weaknesses—and we believe people will actually identify with and respect you more when you recognize your weaknesses.

The process of self-awareness begins by seeking feedback and really listening to it—not thinking about how you're going to respond, but really listening. You'll know you truly listened to feedback if you find yourself challenging your old ways of thinking and behaving; this process can make you feel naked. Alpha personalities, in particular, do not like feeling vulnerable. They're accustomed to people coming to them for answers, not the other way around. They feel that leadership requires confidence and therefore if they doubt themselves, they are failing as leaders.

There's a difference between confidence and conviction. If you have the conviction that you want to be the best leader possible, you will come to understand the need to make yourself vulnerable, seeing that as something that doesn't mean a loss of confidence. True confidence is built on a foundation of self-awareness, and that includes acknowledging your doubts. Don't ignore those moments of uncertainty; investigate them. They may hold valuable lessons that can fuel your growth as a leader. Embrace the process of questioning and learning, and watch your confidence soar.

This is personal work. We've had friends say to us, "It sounds like you want leaders to become better people." Yes, exactly! We believe this work will help you be a better person—which will make you a better leader. That will also make everyone on your team better leaders and improve the experience of everyone in the organization. The whole enterprise will rise when leaders individually rise; we truly believe it.

While self-reflection is valuable, it's limited by our own perspectives. External input helps us break free from our echo chambers, where our own perceptions can dominate.

To gain true self-awareness, we need others to offer insights and challenge our assumptions. Here are some of the most effective ways to gain that valuable outside perspective.

MIRRORS VERSUS SYCOPHANTS

Sycophantic cultures may exist even without narcissists at the top. In any transactional relationship, sycophants are the perfect partners. They are doing a job for money, and therefore recognize that the best use of their role is to do whatever is wanted by the person writing the checks. This is the classic kind of "yes man" who doesn't want to rock the boat and simply carries out the bosses' wishes. Sycophants believe they're playing it safe, but their choices are actually selfish. They're out for themselves, to make their lives easier and their paychecks consistent or bigger. When people are only saying, "Yes," you should ask what their agenda is because it's likely not to help you or support you.

A sycophant in the mail room may not be much danger to a company; however, a sycophant in a senior position can do real harm to an organization. The higher up a sycophant is in an organization, the higher the cost is likely to be to the company and the less respect they will likely receive. The inverse of a sycophant is the highly respected person who acts as a mirror, the person willing to speak truth to power in the spirit of making the organization better, the person giving honest feedback, based on their perception, their experience, and where they think the organization needs to go.

If you have a smudge of ketchup on your face from eating a hot dog and look in a mirror, your reflection in the mirror is not going to hide the smudge from you to avoid hurting your feelings. Think of someone who's not afraid to tell you the hard truth, even if it's a bit embarrassing—like a coworker who'd pull you aside to let you know you have ketchup on your face before a big presentation. They're acting as a mirror, reflecting a reality you can't see yourself, and ultimately helping you and the business.

If you aren't yet utilizing mirrors, you will want to seek them out. You may well already have mirrors around you, and you either aren't recognizing them or aren't empowering them to give you feedback. You will need to create a safe space, so people feel they have permission to speak and tell the truth from their perspective. That won't happen overnight, but you can develop a safe space slowly.

First, name the behavior you seek. Explain that you want people to give you candid feedback. You could communicate something like, "Your insights are important to me. If you have a different perspective on a decision, please share it, whether publicly or privately." Additionally, you can ask them to help you establish parameters and protocols around such conversations, so they'll feel safe, and you can start small, perhaps by asking for honest feedback about the coffee or Friday catered lunches. Start with decisions that are typically contested yet are not important to the organization in the big picture. That way, you are guaranteed to get feedback (people have so many opinions about coffee and lunch) but are not likely to feel defensive.

THE ABSENCE OF LIES IS NOT THE SAME AS THE PRESENCE OF TRUST.

Every time you respond without defensiveness, the space becomes safer as people slowly trust you more. You can't give the person providing feedback any backlash, whether that's by taking a punitive measure or otherwise appearing annoyed. The more evidence you present of taking feedback without giving backlash, the more people will trust you. In our work, many leaders, or those who think they are leaders, tell us, "Everyone in the organization trusts me because I don't lie." They assume that an absence of lies is the same as the presence of trust. That's simply not the case. We can think of plenty of people who tell the truth from their perspective whom we don't trust.

A step up from candid conversations about coffee might be to ask coworkers, "If you were CEO for the day, what are three things you would change about the organization?" Most of the time, people can come up with three ideas right off the bat, but you have to actually be willing to take their ideas and shift policy, or at least, after due consideration, explain with kindness and restraint why you can't enact their ideas. Of course, part of the parameters you'll set will be to let people know that this conversation isn't a genie's lamp granting them three wishes. Still, if you're ultimately going to ignore everyone's ideas, they'll think the whole endeavor is bullshit. (And if you feel yourself silently negating every suggestion, ask yourself why.)

Seeking feedback like this will empower the mirrors who have always been around you to start speaking up. Some leaders also like to seek mirrors outside of the organization. That's fine, but we have caveats. Be cognizant of agendas that might exist for corporate coaches. Remember that advice from people in your "mastermind group" may not directly translate to your enterprise, and know that your drinking buddies only see certain facets of your personality. Keep in mind the context of your relationship in order to really understand the feedback you receive. Having a variety of mirrors from different parts of your life can certainly give you a fuller picture.

You might want to keep a journal, or certainly a mental record of some sort, to record the behaviors people point out to you so they stay top of mind. Furthermore, you can start to think about how the behaviors manifest themselves in a professional versus a personal context. For example, how does stubbornness at home differ from the way stubbornness shows itself at work?

Common themes will pop up; these may well be the first behaviors you'll want to address. Once you've identified them, that can be a natural way to open a conversation with a mirror. If you can identify a quote-unquote negative trait about yourself, and ask their opinion on it, that removes some of the fear factor for the mirror. At least they know they won't be the first person to tell you you're a stubborn SOB.

STACIE'S MIRROR

I used to believe that good leaders projected an image of unwavering strength. This belief was challenged when I managed a highly sensitive employee. My attempts to provide constructive feedback often left her feeling defeated. A colleague's suggestion to show vulnerability completely changed my perspective. I decided to share with the employee a story of a past failure. It felt uncomfortable at first, but the results were remarkable. It created a space for genuine connection and allowed me to get through to her in a way I hadn't been able to before. That experience taught me the unexpected power of vulnerability in leadership.

ERIC'S MIRROR

We all have blind spots in how we communicate. Mine was a tendency to get overly passionate about unimportant things. A friend's honest feedback helped me see this, and it transformed my approach to interactions. Now, I consciously step back when I catch myself getting carried away, and I allow others to express their own ideas. This experience taught me the immense value of feedback and the importance of creating space for diverse perspectives.

THE 360 REVIEW

If you're trying to find your weaknesses and blind spots, a new spin on the traditional 360 Review is a great way to start. Dozens of software packages offer traditional 360 Reviews, wherein an employee's work style is rated via lengthy questionnaires sent to superiors, peers, and subordinates. When you apply that same idea to leadership strengths and weaknesses, you create a powerful tool.

We've created our own 360-style assessment tools (available at mstratpartners.com) to help you gain a clearer picture of your leadership impact. These tools gather feedback on your hard and soft skills, using a one-to-five scale that measures areas like respect, communication, and professional value. The results can pinpoint areas for improvement and highlight potential cultural issues within your team. With a larger sample size, you gain a more objective view of your leadership effectiveness.

To understand the responses to your review in context, you can do our assessment for everyone in the organization, across the board. This will show you more of the general organizational perspective about your culture. For example, if everyone gets low marks for kindness, you may be in a highly transactional environment where there's no value in displaying kindness. This will also help you identify areas you need to work on organizationally, not just individually. We recommend seeking reviews consistently, somewhere between annually and quarterly.

We are big fans of the 360 Review. It's a great way to use subjective inputs to develop an objective way to ensure the little guy in a corporation has a voice with the big guy. Unfortunately, some firms that have implemented 360 Reviews will stop using them the moment a principal doesn't get a high 360-Review score; sadly, that's very common. It's a shame. The 360 Review is an opportunity for you as a professional to improve. Anyway, there's nothing to fear: from what we've seen, someone who actually cares about people rarely gets a poor score.

ERIC'S BRUSH WITH A 360

When I receive feedback, I focus on the areas where I need to improve. I used to get dinged for timeliness, which surprised me. After some reflection, I realized I was overcommitting myself by always saying "yes" to requests, even when my workload was heavy. The solution was simple: I started providing realistic time frames for completing tasks, allowing others to plan accordingly. This improved my efficiency and reduced stress for everyone involved.

STACIE'S BRUSH WITH A 360

In a 360 Review, I received surprisingly negative feedback from a team I rarely interacted with. Rather than dismiss it, I saw an opportunity. I realized that even indirect perceptions mattered. To address this, I organized a lunch with the team to connect on a personal level. This simple gesture allowed us to build rapport and address any misconceptions. It was important to me because I believe in fostering positive relationships throughout the organization, regardless of reporting structures. By taking the initiative, I ensured that my impact on the firm's culture was positive and supportive.

AFTER-ACTION REPORTS

In the military, following a mission, officers want to objectively determine what did and didn't work. In fact, they get extraordinarily verbose about it. After-action reports follow a specific format and ask respondents to state the objective, the result, what went well, and what went wrong, among other data points. We believe in implementing after-action reports in business contexts as well. For example, if you're going into a new market, following the launch, you might ascertain what worked and didn't work by drilling down into a variety of subdecisions you made along the way. After-action reports are also a great door opener for feedback from others in the organization.

After-action reports can include specific questions to guide feedback, such as: "Was the decision appropriate and effective?" "Should the leader have consulted more with others?" "What could be done differently next time?" This structured approach provides valuable insights for leadership development. After-action reports can even be used to assess less-tangible aspects of workplace culture. For instance, if a colleague experiences a family loss, a post-event reflection could gauge the leadership team's response. Did enough people attend the funeral? Does the team prioritize supporting employees during difficult times? This type of reflection encourages open dialogue and allows for adjustments to create a more empathetic and supportive environment.

In this scenario, the colleague who lost a family member is unlikely to approach leadership to say their feelings were hurt that no one from the office attended the funeral. Further, such a scenario sets a precedent for future funerals. So an after-action report may be the only way to analyze that situation in an effort to keep the culture from becoming toxic.

The point is that this hypothetical funeral was an opportunity for leadership to demonstrate care for someone in the organization, but they didn't. An after-action report can help them figure out why and how to show more care next time. This might sound like a strange scenario to plug into an official report—and that is part of our point. These conversations aren't otherwise happening. Enterprises aren't thinking to examine whether or not people attend colleague-family funerals, what the fallout from such a failure might be (a sad and unproductive colleague in the micro and a developing toxic culture in the macro), and how to ensure that a more caring response occurs in the future. It seems incredibly unlikely that someone in leadership would respond to such a questionnaire by saying they don't care when someone's family member passes away, so wouldn't you want to know how and why no one attended? Maybe respondents will say they did care but thought someone else was going to attend in their stead. Maybe they have childhood trauma around funerals and can't attend, even though they empathize deeply with their colleague. Each of those two situations has an easy solution: organize in advance to find out who will attend the funeral, or find an alternative way to demonstrate care besides attending. But those solutions can't be explored unless these conversations are had. After-action reports help you approach such scenarios in an institutionalized and rigorous way.

We're huge proponents of after-action reports, so much so that we believe they have value beyond group settings. Consider using them for personal reflection too. Try this: After an important interaction, jot down some notes in a notebook. Reflect on what went well, what didn't, and how the other person reacted. This "mini after-action report" can help you identify areas for improvement.

We also encourage what we jokingly call "long-after-action reports." Take some time to analyze key interactions from your professional past, even those from years ago. Reflect on how you might have handled those situations differently for a more constructive outcome. You could even seek feedback from those involved, though most of this reflection will likely be solo.

HURDLES

The first barrier to self-reflection is thinking you don't need to do it. It's the classic addict's problem: recognizing there's a need is the first step. That impulse—thinking you don't need self-reflection—is ultimately a defense mechanism, and you can expect to feel it several times throughout the process. Self-reflection is ongoing. It's a journey that never ends, just like leadership.

You'll have to come out of your comfort zone. It can be painful to receive critical feedback, even when offered constructively and with care. It's unpleasant to hear others disagree with your opinions and choices. When you feel uncomfortable, you'll have to fight the urge to justify the behaviors called into question. You'll have to remember the larger goal of getting the best out of your people and your enterprise.

Ego and a desire to cling to power may well be your biggest inhibitors. Many in authority believe, *If I'm the boss, it's my business, so I dictate what happens.* That's like the old joke about the Golden Rule: the one with the gold makes the rule. While that's one way to approach controlling people, it certainly isn't leadership—and it makes you a "boss," not a leader. Anyway, if that's your view, you wouldn't have read this far into the book. Still, you may struggle to dig through the many layers ego inhabits.

Plenty of people attend conferences, read books, and do some amount of self-reflection but barely scratch the surface, all while convincing themselves they're doing the work—or that there's very little work to be done. Hopefully you'll find you're able to dig deeper. This is potentially the most important piece of Invested Leadership. It can be really difficult to self-identify your shortcomings, and, often, you're powerless to do this by yourself. You need help.

It won't be easy. If you are not already accustomed to feedback and self-reflection, you're going to have to grow. It can be scary to empower someone to tell you what they think—especially if they're going to tell you potentially hurtful things that will be hard to hear. You'll have to fight the urge to react defensively: to justify the behavior you feel is being attacked, or, worse, to punish the messenger.

You will want to fight those urges, because the very best leaders understand the value of honest feedback. Even just the first step of identifying a blind spot is a win. And when you overcome a weakness, you'll feel stronger than ever. If you decide you can't or won't overcome a weakness, you can pull in others around you to fill it—which wouldn't happen if you couldn't first identify the weakness. If you utilize the three evaluators explored above—mirrors, 360 Reviews, and after-action reports—you ought to have a fulsome picture of where you excel and where you maybe need some work.

* * *

Self-reflection has amazing benefits. As you start examining your own actions and motivations, others may well notice. Sharing your journey may even inspire them to do the same, creating a ripple effect of positive change. To amplify this impact, encourage your leadership team and potential leaders within your organization to embrace self-reflection. We'll dive deeper into this next.

KEY TAKEAWAYS

- Self-reflection is the first and most important step toward Invested Leadership. Once you know your strengths and weaknesses, you will know how to build out your approach and build up your team.
- Seek out mirrors for honest feedback and avoid sycophants who act selfishly.
- Engage in regular 360 Reviews to help ascertain both personal and organization-wide blind spots.
- After-action reports will ensure you have conversations about issues that might otherwise be swept under the rug.
- Know that ego will continually impede your progress and be prepared to quiet it.

"Surround yourself with the dreamers and the doers...those who see the greatness within you, even when you don't see it yourself."

—ANONYMOUS

"The only way to have a friend is to be one."

—RALPH WALDO EMERSON

"The best mirror is an old friend."

—GEORGE HERBERT

"An honest answer is the sign of true friendship."

—PROVERBS 24:26 (GOOD NEWS TRANSLATION)

"A true friend is someone who thinks that you are a good egg even though he knows that you are slightly cracked."

—BERNARD MELTZER

"Friends show their love in times of trouble, not in happiness."

—EURIPIDES

CHAPTER 4

YOUR TEAM THROUGH NEW EYES

"If you change the way you look at things, the things you look at change."

—WAYNE DYER

We once worked with a firm with a senior executive who had ample subject-matter expertise in many areas, but operations was not one of them. It was universally recognized among management that this senior executive needed an operational person underneath her to support her ability to run the organization. When we looked at the firm, two people stood out who could potentially step into that role.

One had been at the firm significantly longer, had deep institutional knowledge, and was thought to be the "top gun" operator. The other, Diana, was less experienced and possessed less specific operations knowledge. Yet Diana had the edge because of her ability to relate to people—that being specifically what the senior executive lacked, and therefore what the organization needed in this new role it was creating. Diana got the job and quickly caught up in operational knowledge. Meanwhile, she worked to deepen her emotional-intelligence skills. She did so well in the position—excelled because of her blend of EQ and operational-building skills—that she was eventually promoted to become the senior executive's peer.

Years back, the idea of blending EQ skills into operational management was not a thought in many organizations—certainly not in law firms. Typically, operations functioned in a cramdown fashion: a president/CEO/principal spoke, and an operations executive crammed it through. Not Diana; she innovated. For example, to make the ordering of medical records more efficient, the senior executive had recommended having everyone work an extra two hours a day to generate more "work product" (legal term). Diana pushed back, arguing not only that this would be hated by the staff, but that such a tone-deaf cramdown would ultimately diminish productivity.

Diana thought of another way to accomplish the same goal. She developed an asynchronous team by finding an overseas vendor able to supplement the US workforce. This asynchronous team began assisting with the work of ordering medical records. This got the work done faster without taxing the paralegals, while also saving the firm money by avoiding the overtime for paralegals to work ten-hour days. Pushback, even in the form of innovation, rarely occurred previously, and certainly not coupled with a motivation to make something easier for the team—at least not at this organization.

Diana's success wasn't just about her sharp mind or attention to detail. It was her emotional intelligence that truly set her apart. The president tasked her with difficult initiatives, and she consistently delivered, exceeding expectations. She knew how to navigate the human element: building consensus, caring for her team, and motivating them to achieve remarkable results, even in the face of challenging changes. This unique ability to connect with people and inspire them to action was the key to her meteoric rise from entry-level to senior executive.

COLLECTIVE STRENGTHS AND WEAKNESSES

The evaluations we discussed in the last chapter—mirrors, the 360 Review and after-action reports—will also help you identify the leadership skills that already exist in your organization. For most leaders, they only have their own perspective on colleagues, usually based solely on their own interactions with them. They see a different person than their subordinates see.

We've had several clients who were repeatedly surprised by the opinions people on his leadership team had about specific people within the organization. They had a completely different impression of the employees in question—but of course they did! Interactions from the top down are very different from peer-to-peer interactions.

Knowing your staff—their strengths, weaknesses, and how they work together—is crucial for effective team management. This deep understanding allows you to:

- Identify and address team-wide vulnerabilities.
- Strategically recruit talent to fill skill gaps.
- Optimize team performance by leveraging individual strengths.

To gain this valuable insight, utilize the assessment tools from the last chapter: mirrors, 360 Reviews, and after-action reports.

It is important to keep these evaluations separate from your own evaluations as a principal; there's a reason we didn't combine this chapter with the previous one. If the principal's self-evaluation happens in a group setting, it's too easy for the principal to do minimal reflection and nevertheless feel like they've checked a box, so we wanted to keep this chapter separate. Also, there's more to discuss about team-wide evaluations than what was covered in the last chapter. That said, this chapter will be shorter than the others.

TITLE DOES NOT CONVEY LEADERSHIP.

QUEEN BEES

Through the process of team-wide self-reflection, you may also discover existing natural leaders in your organization who may not necessarily be in positions of authority. Who are people flocking to for advice about personal situations? Who is constantly helping others? Those are displays of leadership. They may not yet be in formal positions of leadership within your organization, but make no mistake, they are leaders.

The military concept of winning hearts and minds speaks to the idea of gaining the trust of the populace of a community—more specifically, it speaks to winning the natural leaders within the populace. When you have those people, everyone else who looks to them will follow. The inverse is also true: your employees won't follow somebody just because you name them a manager. They may have to follow these managers' directions due to their position of authority, but they will continue following the naturally acting leaders in their peer group—it's the difference between management and leadership.

When we evaluate client firms, particularly law firms, we look for the role we call the "Queen Bee." The Queen Bee can be male or female—the title only conveys that the person holds the most powerful position in the proverbial hive. In a law firm, they are often in the seat of power or very close to it. The Queen Bee in a law firm is typically a senior nonattorney (usually a present or prior paralegal) who has been there seemingly forever. Typically, this person has been keeping the trains moving for years. They monitor processes and make sure everything happens at the prescribed time. They are usually in a classic managerial role, not necessarily a leadership role. If we go into a law firm and try to institute changes—cultural, operational, really anything—and we don't have buy-in from the Queen Bee, we fail every time. Why? Often, it is due to the fact that this person is considered by the staff to be as much of a leader as the principal is. The Queen Bee's influence is undeniable. Followers may respect this person's judgment, succumb to the pressure of this person's popular views, or simply act out of fear.

Title does not convey leadership. You could be a vice president, but if no one in your charge thinks you're a leader, you're just a boss. People may do what you say because you have the purse strings, but they wouldn't necessarily trust or follow you in a crisis. The inverse is also true; in a crisis, your people will follow whomever they do trust. We think plenty of people will read this book who are those nascent natural leaders in organizations, what we call cultural leaders. (Perhaps you, the reader, are one of them, someone hoping to grow as a leader and develop your skills.) Culture leaders can absolutely change the course of an organization by swaying negativity or positivity, by providing buy-in.

To successfully implement their initiatives, principals need to secure buy-in from key individuals. It is surprising how often this reality is ignored. The fact is, the unofficial "cultural leaders" often wield significant influence among their peers, regardless of their formal titles. These individuals typically emerge because of their genuine concern for others, which naturally attracts people to their perspective. Principals should identify and collaborate with these cultural leaders to effectively drive project success and foster a supportive environment. Giving a shit about people is actually very, very powerful; it could make anyone a de facto leader. In this way, leadership develops organically, genuinely, and authentically. Titles and authority don't guarantee genuine care for people—in fact, the opposite is often true. True influence comes from earning the trust and respect of others. By recognizing and empowering those who genuinely care, and amplifying their voices within the organization, you can create positive change. Giving a shit about people, coupled with know-how, can result in a well-run, efficient, KPI-enhanced, maximally successful enterprise that will mow down its competitors every day of the week and twice on Sunday.

BAD FOR THE HIVE

Maestro was engaged by a small law firm aiming for rapid growth. We began, as usual, with confidential interviews across all staff levels. We quickly discovered that the firm's office manager, while outwardly pleasant, exerted an unhealthy level of control over the environment, dictating everything from footwear to bathroom breaks.

The owner, though aware of this dynamic, was hesitant to challenge her authority, believing her to be crucial to the firm's operations. Fearful of her leaving the firm, he insisted that all changes be approved by her. We carefully presented our initial recommendations, but the office manager, feeling threatened, quickly undermined the plan.

We emphasized to the owner that her cooperation was essential for success. She needed to champion his vision and our strategy. Unfortunately, she resisted every step, prioritizing her own power and a "we've always done it that way" mentality over the firm's needs. Because the owner overestimated her value and lived in constant fear of her departure, he failed to intervene effectively.

Ultimately, Maestro had to withdraw from the project, recognizing our inability to succeed without the office manager's support. We refunded the remaining fees and ended the relationship. Honestly, we felt bad for the owner—he was in a prison of his own making.

THE PREDICTIVE INDEX

When identifying potential leaders who complement your strengths and fill your leadership gaps, consider leveraging tools like the Predictive Index. This powerful psychometric assessment delves into a candidate's work style, personality, and behavioral tendencies, providing a data-driven understanding of their potential.

The Predictive Index offers several key advantages:

- Objective insights: It goes beyond surface-level impressions, offering an objective assessment of an individual's strengths, blind spots, and motivations. This data helps you understand how they might operate in various leadership scenarios.
- Self-awareness versus reality: By comparing an individual's self-perception to the assessment results, you can identify potential disconnects. This reveals areas for growth and helps you understand if they have a realistic view of their own capabilities.
- Targeted candidate searches: Need someone with specific traits? The Predictive Index allows you to search for candidates who possess similar or contrasting attributes to existing team members or even yourself. This is invaluable for building balanced and effective leadership teams.

However, while the Predictive Index is a powerful tool, it should be used in conjunction with other methods:

- 360 Reviews: Gather feedback from a candidate's peers and colleagues to understand their reputation and how they are perceived by others.
- Personal observation: Your own experiences and observations of the candidate in action provide valuable context and insight.

By combining the objective data from the Predictive Index with qualitative feedback and your own judgment, you can make more informed decisions about identifying and developing future leaders.

KEY TAKEAWAYS

The process of self-reflection should be extended to your leadership team and throughout the entire organization.

To avoid blind spots within your leadership team, ascertain their collective strengths and weaknesses. This will also help you determine who can fill your own blind spots.

Such a process will further identify natural cultural leaders and their skillsets within the wider organization.

Seek mirrors, execute company-wide 360 Reviews, encourage after-action reports, and utilize the Predictive Index among the leadership team and other cultural leaders.

"Coming together is a beginning. Keeping together is progress. Working together is success."

—HENRY FORD

"You never really understand a person until you consider things from his point of view."

—ATTICUS FINCH, *To Kill a Mockingbird* BY HARPER LEE

"Empathy begins with understanding life from another person's perspective. Nobody has an objective experience of reality. It's all through our own individual prisms."

—STERLING K. BROWN

"Everything is only an impression."

—MARCUS AURELIUS, *MEDITATIONS*

"Perspective is everything when you are experiencing the challenges of life."

—ANONYMOUS

CHAPTER 5

THE ROI OF CARING

"Everyone you hire is so important. You assume that every switch-board operator will excel, and they will. Often people make mistakes, but you allow for that, too. Praise people—like plants, they must be nurtured—and make it fun. Value them and give them the opportunity to contribute in ways that excite them...Keep it vibrant. Everything comes back to people. Nothing else. You get loyalty, enthusiasm, and great service for your customers."

—RICHARD BRANSON[10]

A quick Google search of Richard Branson reveals his unwavering commitment to his employees. In fact, he champions a philosophy that could seem counterintuitive at first: prioritizing employees over customers. While this might sound like heresy in the business world, Branson firmly believes that happy, engaged employees naturally translate to satisfied customers. He argues that by focusing

---

10   David Sheff, "Richard Branson: The Interview," Forbes, February 24, 1997, archived at https://www.davidsheff.com/richard-branson-two.

on creating a positive and supportive environment for your team, you empower them to provide exceptional service, ultimately achieving customer satisfaction organically.

This approach reflects a deeper understanding of leadership. As a CEO, your primary responsibility isn't to directly handle every customer interaction. Instead, your focus should be on cultivating a thriving workforce equipped to meet customer needs. By investing in your employees' well-being, professional development, and overall satisfaction, you create a culture where they are genuinely motivated to go above and beyond for your customers. Branson's famous quote, "Train people well enough so they can leave; treat them well enough so they don't want to," perfectly encapsulates this philosophy.

Branson does this in a variety of ways. He offers on-site gyms and casual dress codes and generally creates an office culture people enjoy coming in for and participating in. There are also anecdotes about Branson in the trenches with his employees, such as dressing as a flight attendant. There are stories that, in the early days, when flights were cancelled and passengers were stuck, he joined his employees at the ticketing counter, going so far as to sleep on the floor beside them and the stranded travelers. This act of solidarity underscored his empathy and willingness to share in their discomfort. That kind of leadership tells people they are all cared for equally, and they're all in this together.

Such togetherness includes access. At the end of a monthly letter Branson writes to more than five thousand employees, he includes his telephone number and home address. You might think he gets flooded with phone calls about petty interpersonal problems, but in practice, giving employees such a privilege is a way of respecting them, which leads them in turn to respect Branson's time. He reports that people almost always write instead of call (he receives about forty letters a day and ensures they are all answered).

Further, when supervisors know their direct reports can reach Branson anytime about anything, they're on their best behavior as well. "I gently respect the role of the supervisors, but I will look at any problems that arise. The people in charge know that; it makes them much more caring as a result," he explains.[11]

Richard Branson prioritizes employee care by building trust. His unlimited vacation policy exemplifies this, recognizing that trusted employees, invested in the company's mission, won't abuse it. He encourages risk-taking and views mistakes as learning opportunities, fostering a culture of innovation. Branson champions open communication, valuing employee feedback and creating a safe space for sharing ideas. By building trust, Branson empowers his employees, creating a motivated and engaged workforce dedicated to achieving remarkable things. When care is invested authentically, the return always comes.

MORE THAN A WIDGET

Invested Leaders understand their employees are not simply parts of the company machine but are individuals, and every human is multifaceted. Your employee is also somebody's child, parent, or spouse. If you insist that an employee automatically elevates one of your priorities over the other facets of their life (insisting on evening hours or

---

11   Sheff, "Branson."

weekend work), you create conflict. On a superficial level, such a decree is impractical: shit happens to all of us, and we can't always schedule it for after 5:00 p.m., but fundamentally, consistently expecting someone to ignore (or place in secondary positions) the other facets of their life will undermine their belief that you care for them, which sows seeds of distrust. Any business may sometimes ask more of its team—what you don't want is for your people to assume, in such a moment, that you don't respect them enough to value their family time and outside interests. When you've built a foundation of genuine caring, your people will instead see extreme asks as evidence of true need; they'll want to help rather than feeling like you're just trying to squeeze more juice out of a turnip.

At Maestro, if we hired you, we basically said we trust you. We don't want a culture where we're asking an employee why there's a Starbucks charge on the company card. If you were getting ready to go on-site with a client and want to stop for a cup of coffee, we choose to believe that was going to make you better equipped to meet the client. We have to believe you understand the overall goal of the company and make choices that align with it. If you want to have drinks after a gig, we're not going to micromanage that. If we couldn't trust you with a credit card, we shouldn't have hired you.

THE CURRENCY OF CARE: INVESTING IN TRUST

Trust is everything—it's binary; there's no middle ground. You either have it or you don't. Trust is the foundation for everything. Building trust is essential to caring for employees. In fact, it's the ultimate expression of that care. When employees truly feel trusted, they'll do anything for you and the company. Even so, such a relationship could never lead to abuse, because that would inherently betray trust, and the relationship would collapse. That's why we used the term ROI in the title of this chapter: think of caring as an investment. It's one you have to make without expecting a return, or else it will be inauthentic. But when care is invested authentically, the return always comes.

Again, trust is everything. It's binary; there's no middle ground. You either have it or you don't. How do you build it? By avoiding micromanagement, yes, and most important, by caring for your employees. That's what we'll focus on now. Here are the most impactful ways to exercise and show care in an organization.

LISTEN

Listening is not the same thing as being quiet while someone speaks. We've all had a boss who asks how your weekend was even though both of you know the reason they came to your desk was to ask for a report and literally the moment you finish the sentence of what happened that weekend, your boss went right into the report. That's not listening. That's lip service toward the idea of a conversation—which not only wasted time but may well have communicated that they do not actually care.

BEING PRESENT AND ACTUALLY LISTENING IS THE SAME THING AS LOOKING FOR OPPORTUNITIES TO CARE.

To be clear, everyone in leadership doesn't have to ask everyone else how their weekends were. In fact, if it's going to be lip service, it's better that you don't. When you do ask a question, make it count. When someone knocks on your door to share, pay attention and be present. It sounds like common sense, but it is woefully rare in corporate culture. That's why it can be so radical to listen with intention rather than doing it just to check a box. That's why it feels transformative to be present so you can actually take in and respond to what's said rather than simply hearing it.

Many think they know what it means to intentionally listen with presence, but they still miss the bar. Here's the best way we can describe the distinction: being present and actually listening is the same thing as looking for opportunities to care. Actual listening is noticing opportunities to connect and ways to help. Actual listening creates actual safe spaces, where employees feel they will be listened to without retribution rather than feeling resentment toward disingenuous efforts. When you approach a conversation that way, you will feel the difference, we promise.

ERIC ON LISTENING

I was responsible for the claims administration for the plaintiffs of one of the largest civil-rights class actions in US history. It was a crazy time, a nonstop fire hose of work. In the middle of the madness, one day, one of my managers came into my office and asked a question about one of his subordinates: "Are you and Tommy friends? Do you hang out?" I found the question absurd, and basically brushed it off, saying "No. I barely know the guy." Then I got back to work.

Several weeks later, I learned that another team member, Sabrina, had been allowing Tommy free use of a company vehicle for personal reasons. It had been going on for months. Everyone assumed it was happening with my consent. And that was creating bad feelings and jealousy, in the ways that favoritism always does. In retrospect, I saw that the manager who had entered my office weeks prior had been walking a tightrope, trying to tip me off to the situation without implicating himself in the gossip. He had been looking out for me because people were starting to talk about it, but I had been too busy to hear it. Had I taken the time to jump off the conveyor belt and be present—to really listen and to ask more questions related to "why" he thought that—I would have learned about the scheme and saved the team a lot of heartburn. I also would have made that manager feel valued and appreciated.

RESPECT

People think a lot about respecting leaders, but the reality is that everyone wants respect. Everyone in your company wants to feel their role has at least a modicum of importance and is respected. One of the most basic ways a leader can respect those in their charge is to create a pleasant, if not genuinely happy and safe, work environment. If you believe your business is important, the next question to ask is whether people are important to your business. If that answer is yes—and we can't imagine a scenario in which it's not—it makes sense to create a positive environment for your people. You not only need to employ the best people for them to be successful, but you also need them to be happy and engaged.

Leadership also shows respect by engaging in behavior that suggests "we're in this together." The Marine Corps uses the term "gung ho." The phrase derives from a Chinese term roughly translating to "work together" and became a Marine Corps hallmark thanks to Lieutenant Colonel Evans Carlson. He was deeply impressed by the collaborative spirit it fostered within the Chinese army before World War II, and he incorporated this philosophy into his own unit, the forerunners of today's special operations unit, the Marine Raiders. A leader who is not too good to do things they would ask of those in their charge is the epitome of "we're in this together" and also likely has a far greater understanding of the role and responsibilities of their team. A leader's willingness to get their hands dirty is perhaps one of the best ways to engender two-way respect.

Another way to demonstrate care through respect is as simple as believing in people. I'm sure when some of you were kids, you had parents who said you could do anything—and you trusted and internalized that. You kept it in your back pocket when you felt challenged and used it to overcome. You can achieve a hell of a lot when someone believes in you. It builds confidence. This dynamic is absolutely transferable to the workplace—in fact, that's precisely where it can be most evident.

MANY IMAGINE LEADERSHIP TO BE A CROWN, BUT IT'S MORE LIKE A HEAVY CLOAK OF RESPONSIBILITY.

SHARE THE BURDEN

Stacie learned this lesson in her father's warehouse, after witnessing him pick up the slack whenever the people he managed fell behind. Eric learned this lesson in the Marines, where no one was too good to do the basic work of others when necessary. Sharing someone's burden, or taking it off of them, is one of the most fundamental ways humans show care for one another, regardless of the context. It can look like leadership manning the phone lines after an emergency, sending the receptionist home. Or it can look like buying groceries for a single-mom paralegal after hearing through the grapevine that she struggled that month due to unexpected expenses.

When you're sharing the burden of others, you show that you see them and understand their circumstances. It demonstrates that you care about their individual success. It also exemplifies your commitment to the business and its mission, which will further energize the crew. The phrase "not my job" is one of the top ways businesses die (another is "we've always done it this way"). In times of need, leaders roll up their sleeves and do what needs to be done to help those in the organization who need to be helped.

Many imagine leadership to be a crown, but it's more like a heavy cloak of responsibility. Ascending the leadership ladder doesn't always mean escaping the mundane. In fact, the higher you climb, the more you might find yourself returning to those seemingly insignificant tasks, or at the very least, ensuring resources are dedicated to them. True leadership often involves recognizing the importance of every role and taking ultimate responsibility for the success of the whole, not just the glamorous parts.

WHAT LOOKS LIKE CARE BUT ISN'T

Caring does not equal friendship; people often conflate the two. That's a problem. If somebody on the street trips and falls, and you help them up and check to see if you can call them an ambulance or an Uber, that's a way of caring for that person, but they're not your friend. You don't even know their name. In our careers, the people we've worked with know we care about them, but that was never confused as friendship.

Keep the brightest line and clearest gap between professional and friendly relationships. Friendships come with certain expectations that business relationships don't have the latitude to meet. For example, if I am your manager, and you're continually late to work because of childcare issues, I could dictate that punitive measures be taken or, if I actually care about you, I might tell you to bring your kid to work or I might arrange a ride for your kid, but those latter actions would not suggest I am your friend. We once donated to a GoFundMe for a staff member whose son's house burned down, and he had eleven kids. We can think of a lot of friends to whom we've never given $250.

STACIE ON AVOIDING "FRIENDSHIP"

At a firm where I previously worked, I was charged with taking over a department that had become a total mess. It was viewed as the worst team at the firm at the time. They were in the throes of disaster, largely resulting from the actions of a prior manager, who was then leaving the firm. I knew how she had managed the team, so in my speech, on the first day I met with them, I announced, "I will not be going clubbing with you."

The prior manager took them out clubbing all the time. They all became friends. They loved her, but they took advantage of it, of course, as most people would. After big nights out, some would call in hungover, and she would cover for them, explaining that they had gotten sick. At first, when I took over the team, I was unpopular. I told them that, even though I was not their friend, I was committed to growing their careers, and we would make this the best department in the firm.

Fast-forward a few months to when I gained their respect and cleaned up the team. At that point, they spoke honestly with me, explaining that they felt their careers were on a better track, and they were much happier with the work they were doing. They admitted that they had not ultimately liked my predecessor's managerial style, even though they had liked her.

Another problem with developing friendships at work: you may have a legal obligation to treat your direct reports equally under the policies of your company. If you're friends with some and not with others, there will always be a color of favoritism to your leadership. That introduces toxicity. Whoever is not invited to the after-work friend hang feels excluded. Worse, they could miss out on workplace information and tactical discussions that happen off-site, leaving them behind and potentially able to make accusations of malfeasance.

THE CARE PEOPLE WANT

We have explored a variety of ways to demonstrate care in the workplace. Regardless of the actions you take, ensure they exemplify how people want to be cared for; otherwise, you're just checking a box. You're doing it for you instead of for them. That, being inauthentic, will backfire. For example, Maestro had a former client whose principal was fond of bringing in pizzas on Friday. It was easy for him to do; in fact, he brought pizza one of the days we were on-site.

Later, during our one-on-one meeting, he shared the story of a time one of his direct reports thanked him for the gesture but spoke up to say she doesn't really eat pizza and would much prefer a salad. In our experience, nine out of ten people receiving that feedback would respond the same way he did: he described her to us as ungrateful. During that moment of feedback from her, he could've taken the opportunity to listen, agree that she made a fair point, recognize that not everybody loves pizza, and grab a couple salads next time he brings lunch. It wouldn't even be an additional bother for him—what pizza place doesn't have salad? It's such an easy fix! By making that one small tweak, suddenly he would've been a hero because he listened. And that's the crux: it's not about the salad or the pizza; it's about listening.

Instead, he took the feedback personally. He saw himself as being benevolent. It wasn't about providing his staff with a treat. He was doing it because he wanted a gold star. Therefore, when she declined his treat, he couldn't get beyond feeling rejected, feeling that his benevolence itself had been negated. The irony of that meeting wasn't lost on me. We, too, would have preferred a salad that day. His dismissive reaction created such a negative atmosphere that it felt impossible to express that simple preference, let alone address the deeper issue: his inability to accept feedback and his fundamental misunderstanding of how to treat employees. His hostility shut down any possibility of productive communication.

EVERYONE IS A LEADER.

As you've likely assumed, learning how those in your charge want to be cared for is as simple as communicating and listening. In that endeavor, certain systems can help.

- First, think about caring in small teams. If you have more than ten direct reports, you should reorganize your structure (one study indicates seven is the optimal number).[12] Focus your caring and intentional listening there. Get to know them and what's important to them. Ask about their likes and dislikes and their hobbies. Learn what resonates with them. Not only will this help you meet the needs of those people, but you'll be modeling caring leadership for them, which they will carry through to their own direct reports (again, ideally ten or fewer people).
- Some companies structure feedback via surveys. They literally ask employees to share not only opinions about

---

12   George A. Miller, "The Magical Number Seven, Plus or Minus Two: Some Limits on Our Capacity for Processing Information," Psychological Review 101, no. 2 (April 1994): 343–352, https://doi.org/10.1037/0033-295X.101.2.343.

the organization but also whether or not they want to play in an office kickball league on Fridays or go bowling once a quarter. We also find helpful what you might call a live survey: when you cater lunch and, while people eat, seek feedback on a variety of topics or open up the floor to a town hall–style Q&A session.

- For our money, though, good, old-fashioned, direct, personal communication is the best path forward. Learning how people want to be cared for ultimately comes down to learning about them as people. Therefore, any conversation will deliver key pieces of information. Set aside time to chat with your direct reports about their lives and interests. You will learn plenty about what they need in order to feel like humans, not just cogs in the machine. Bonus: from conversations like these, you'll also learn how to improve your business, because you'll discover inefficiencies as well as underutilized skillsets. Mitigating the former and mining the latter will both increase your employees' ability to thrive.

- To encourage direct conversation, some leaders institute an "open door" policy, which, to tell you something you already know, basically invites anyone in the organization to pop by for a chat whenever, without needing to schedule in advance. This system isn't for everyone, though. Some (for example, Eric) have a hard time remaining productive through interruptions. If that's you, consider shifting the meaning of the parameters of your "open" policy. Eric keeps his door closed, but everyone knows that when he's out in the halls, he's available for any conversation, question, or suggestion. He says it's an "ears always open" policy.

- Some colleagues and staff members might feel intimidated to share feedback directly with members of a leadership team. To ensure you also hear from them and not only from the organization's squeaky wheels, you could also consider committees that allow employees to share opinions with peers. These people may also respond well to a classic suggestion box (or the surveys).

We are not big fans of anonymous feedback, but we do accept that this is sometimes the only way you'll hear hard truths. Once leaders begin engaging more with feedback, trust will develop, a safe space will be created, and direct personal communication will grow as a result. Even better, throughout the journey of learning how people in your organization want to be cared for, you will also be engaging in that care. Asking questions and receiving feedback is a form of care.

NOW YOU HAVE A CULTURE OF LEADERS

Challenging the traditional notion that leadership is reserved for a select few, we propose a more inclusive view: everyone is a leader. While some might argue that leadership requires followers, we believe that the act of choosing to follow or not is itself an exercise in leadership, particularly when others are influenced by that choice. This creates a dynamic where leadership is constantly being negotiated and shared. Consider our own relationship: while we both embody leadership, the degree to which we exert influence may vary depending on the situation. This doesn't diminish the leadership capacity of either individual but rather highlights the collaborative and contextual nature of true leadership.

One of Invested Leadership's primary goals is to create a culture of leadership. We want to grow everyone in an organization to become leaders themselves to some degree. Some organizations even have rubrics: leadership-development training regimens, wherein employees read books and jump through a certain number of hoops in order to become "anointed" leaders. Those systems certainly provide information toward leadership, but they don't necessarily create leaders. In our opinion, Invested Leadership is the most foundational and transformative way to develop a culture of leadership in an organization.

Once you've created a caring culture and your so-named leaders are truly embodying that culture, you will have a successful company. A group of people who are single minded toward a common goal cannot be defeated.

KEY TAKEAWAYS

- Make sure you care for people in a way they want and need, rather than in a way that makes you feel good about yourself for checking a box.
- Trust is everything. Building trust is a way of caring for employees, and caring for employees is a way of building trust. When you have trust, you can't lose.
- Build trust by intentionally listening, demonstrating authentic respect, and finding ways to recognize what burdens those in your charge and then diminishing those burdens.
- Caring and friendship are not the same thing. Lean into the first without falling into the second.
- Invested Leadership will naturally help you develop a culture of leadership, and that will make your organization bulletproof.

"In leadership, there are no words more important than trust. In any organization, trust must be developed among every member of the team if success is going to be achieved."

—MIKE KRZYZEWSKI

"Employees who believe that management is concerned about them as a whole person—not just an employee—are more productive, more satisfied, more fulfilled. Satisfied employees mean satisfied customers, which leads to profitability."

—ANNE M. MULCAHY

"You can't buy engagement; you have to build engagement."

—ANONYMOUS

"The way your employees feel is the way your customers will feel. And if your employees don't feel valued, neither will your customers."

—SYBIL F. STERSHIC

"The purpose of human life is to serve, and to show compassion and the will to help others."

—ALBERT SCHWEITZER

"The greatest good you can do for another is not just to share your riches but to reveal to him his own."

—BENJAMIN DISRAELI

"The best way to find yourself is to lose yourself in the service of others."

—MAHATMA GANDHI

CHAPTER 6

CHANGE WHAT YOU CAN AND PARTNER TO COVER THE REST

"None of us is as smart as all of us."

—KEN BLANCHARD

If you have investments or pay attention to anything in the financial sector, you likely know of Berkshire Hathaway. The duo behind Berkshire Hathaway was Warren Buffett and Charlie Munger. Though Warren Buffett is famously known as the "Oracle of Omaha," he has enough self-awareness and humility to admit he does not know everything and lacks expertise in certain industries and technologies. This is where Charlie Munger, his longtime business partner, came in. Munger brought a broad knowledge base and a different perspective, often challenging Buffett's assumptions and providing critical insights. Munger's ability to analyze businesses from multiple angles and his focus on risk management complemented Buffett's strengths, making them a formidable team. Their success over decades exemplifies the power of recognizing one's weaknesses and surrounding oneself with people who possess the necessary skills to fill those gaps.

This is perfectly analogous to what this book asks of you. Set aside time on a regular basis to inventory your strengths and weaknesses. Set aside time to learn how those in your charge want to be cared for. Then, set aside time to put that puzzle together. How can you use your skillsets to intentionally care within your organization? When you don't have the skillset for a particular need, can you develop the skillset to fill that need yourself? When that's not possible, who else on your leadership team can fill your pothole? (Or whom can you bring in to do so?)

This process is a form of learning just like any other. Treat it as such, gather the resources you need, and make the time. That is how you'll become an expert in leadership. After all, you didn't come out of the womb that way. Certain leadership traits are natural, yes, but we do not believe one is a "born" leader. As with any skill, leadership requires work and effort. It requires investment.

WHEN AUTHENTICITY IS EVERYTHING

We have written quite a bit about the shortcomings of quote-unquote authentic leadership; however, make no mistake, authenticity as a character trait is absolutely critical in the execution of Invested Leadership. You must be completely honest with yourself and everyone else about what you can and can't achieve in the caring arena. You've taken this inventory of yourself and everyone in your organization to determine strengths and weaknesses when it comes to caring. What happens next?

The first thing you should do is determine whether the forms of care being requested are valid, appropriate, and realistic needs and requests. If Susie likes hugs in the morning, sorry, can't help you, Susie: that's potentially a lawsuit. However, if Susie wants quick, meaningful conversations in the morning, then you have a decision to make. Is that something you can do or not?

To answer this question, you must be your true, authentic self. Maybe you think it's a great idea, and even though you've never done it before, you want to try. If your spirit is pure, and you're trying for the right reasons, even if you're terrible at it, Susie will feel cared for. On the other hand, if you try to engage Susie even though you think a morning conversation with her is counterproductive—or even if you recognize the need but are going to hate it the whole time—your efforts will backfire. That will diminish trust.

Now that you've worked through the previous chapters, you have a lot of data: about your own strengths and weaknesses, and about what your employees want. Now is the time to look at this list and be candid with yourself about what you are and aren't capable of, about what you do and don't want to do. Choose those that you can (or can learn to) tackle personally. Then pull in other leaders to handle the rest.

You don't have to be the person to demonstrate every effort of caring. No one can, so neither can you—that is as authentic as the day is long. Problems only arise when you feel you must be everything to everyone. There's a direct correlation between authenticity and trust. Problems inevitably arise when we attempt to project an image that doesn't align with our true nature. This inauthenticity is a form of falsehood, and falsehoods are fundamentally incompatible with trust.

The quickest way to gut-check whether your efforts at caring are authentic or not is to question your motivation. Do you genuinely want to try to demonstrate care in this way, or are you just checking a box? Or, worse, are you just trying to look like you care to appear benevolent? Your motivation will always be your guide. Checking it will prevent inauthenticity every time.

Remember that deputizing team members to care for your employees is also a way to demonstrate care for your employees. You're ensuring their needs are met, regardless of who meets them. For the rest of this chapter, we're going to explore actionable advice Invested Leaders can use to help implement the data they've gathered thus far.

WHEN YOU FOCUS ON CARING ABOUT YOUR PEOPLE, THAT WILL NECESSARILY DRIVE ENGAGEMENT.

BUY-IN

The foundation of Invested Leadership is agreeing with the hypothesis that caring about people is necessary and positive, both interpersonally and professionally—those are table stakes. If you don't believe that's true, and you're merely trying to reduce turnover, we think you will ultimately fail. We saw an article recently about the importance of focusing on employee engagement. That's like saying a married couple should only focus on not getting divorced; the premise is completely ridiculous.

When you focus on caring about your people, that will necessarily drive engagement. They will reciprocally care about you and the enterprise—if they don't, they were poor cultural fits to begin with. On the other hand, when you focus only on the end, your caring will be inauthentic, and you will lose talent in today's market.

We had a client that was renowned for their laser focus on numbers. Every employee, from the managing partner down to the interns, was evaluated solely based on quantitative metrics: intakes, clients, production, and, of course, profit. The company's motto was "Numbers don't lie." That's all well and good. Metrics are metrics, and law firms need revenue. Regardless, the fact is that you have to focus on numbers in a way that doesn't negatively affect your culture. Unfortunately, this firm did not do that.

Under the regime of the leader at the time, profits soared, but a toxic culture festered under the surface. Employees were overworked, stressed, and constantly afraid of falling short of their targets. Burnout was rampant, and turnover was high. One day, a new managing partner, Sarah, took the helm. Sarah was a visionary leader with a deeper understanding of human psychology. She recognized that the obsession with numbers was stifling creativity, innovation, and employee well-being.

Sarah started having conversations with associates, paralegals, and assistants to explain why each piece of work was important and how it fit into the firm's larger goals. She endeavored to give them a sense of ownership over their tasks, and also worked with employees to evaluate the kinds of cases they each handled, to determine which were more time-consuming than others. She swapped some cases among them to achieve more equitable work distribution, and also gamified some of the metrics, introducing good-natured competition. Her most effective tactic in shifting the firm out of a toxic culture involved a client.

When a firm becomes metrics-focused, it can be tempted to start settling cases just to reach numbers rather than working to get the most for each and every client. Sarah pledged always to do what's in the best interest of the client, regardless of that decision's financial impact on the firm. Shortly thereafter, the case took a turn, and the client ended up not getting enough money. She ate a good portion of the firm's fee in order to put as much money in the client's pocket as possible. Obviously, that's not ideal, but it did have a profound effect. It communicated to the staff and attorneys that she really does care about her clients—meaning, she can be trusted when she says she cares about employees too. In this scenario, Sarah got buy-in from the staff specifically because she had demonstrated buy-in herself.

Employees started to feel valued and appreciated. They were more engaged in their work, and their productivity increased. Creativity and innovation flourished. Turnover decreased, and the firm became an employer of choice. The company's financial performance also improved. The focus on people led to better customer service, stronger relationships with partners, and a more motivated workforce. By shifting its focus from numbers to people, the company created a healthier, more productive, and more successful workplace.

BE ACCOUNTABLE AND VULNERABLE

Consider candidly explaining this process to everyone in your organization. We recognize that won't work in every enterprise (depending on how much trust yet exists in the environment, such a pronouncement may be perceived as manipulative to some people). In our experience, at the end of the day, people respect integrity, candor, and transparency. You might explain that true leaders are always working on themselves, which is why you've been seeking feedback, identifying your potholes, and leaning on your team.

First, this will create accountability. In corporate America, the head of a company is accountable to the board for a variety of results regarding the health of the company. We are just inverting that same idea a bit to recommend you also hold yourself accountable to those quote-unquote beneath you. This can build an incredible amount of trust. Essentially, you're acknowledging that you have something you're developing, and you'll need the help of everyone in the organization to do it.

When you point out a weakness you're working to strengthen, we have found that people will respect and trust you more. When you share your vulnerabilities, those become your greatest strengths. Sharing them will hugely impact people.

There's no way this process won't make you vulnerable to them anyway; receiving and actually hearing feedback requires vulnerability. We truly believe that the greater good is served by the genuine vulnerability of leaders.

Vulnerability isn't about relinquishing control; it's about recognizing that true leadership doesn't lie in controlling others. The most effective leaders don't strive to dominate; they foster trust, connection, and collaboration. Think of your leadership, vision, and destination goals as your products. While it may seem counterintuitive, vulnerability can be the most effective form of control. When you're willing to be vulnerable, you demonstrate a level of confidence and self-assurance that inspires trust and invites connection. This approach stands in stark contrast to the traditional command-and-control style of leadership, which often relies on fear and coercion. True authority comes from within, from the willingness to be open and authentic, not from demanding obedience.

YOU'RE NOT COMPETING WITH OTHER LEADERS. YOU'RE COMPETING WITH THE LEADER YOU WERE YESTERDAY.

Vulnerability is the catalyst that transforms weakness into strength. Imagine a ship setting sail with hidden structural flaws. It might appear strong on the surface, but it's vulnerable to disaster. Similarly, organizations that try to conceal their weaknesses create a facade of strength that can easily crumble under pressure. Identifying weakness allows you all to problem-solve around it and improve. Organizations thrive not by hiding flaws but by addressing them openly. So called "weakness" can lead to strength. After all, bodybuilders are never weaker than after a workout. It is precisely that process of intentionally making their bodies vulnerable that ends up making them stronger.

SELF-COMPETE

Leadership isn't a destination you arrive at; it's a continuous journey of self-discovery and development. It's a path marked by constant evolution, where complacency leads to stagnation. To truly lead, we must embrace the challenge of becoming better versions of ourselves, day after day. This requires a willingness to step outside our comfort zones, to confront our limitations, and to invest in our own growth. It's about betting on ourselves, not in a self-serving way but with a deep commitment to maximizing our potential and positively impacting those around us.

You're not competing with other leaders. You're competing with the leader you were yesterday. It's about striving to surpass our past selves, to learn from our mistakes, and to continually refine our skills and perspectives. This isn't about seeking external validation or comparing ourselves to others; it's about an internal drive to become more authentic, more empathetic, and more effective in our leadership roles. It's about leading with integrity, inspiring those around us, and leaving a positive mark on the world.

HACK RESEARCH

In our quest for continuous improvement as leaders, we often seek out books, workshops, and mentors. While these resources are invaluable, there's a simple yet powerful tool that can significantly amplify our growth: Google Alerts. By setting up alerts for keywords like "leadership" and "emotional intelligence," we open ourselves to a constant stream of relevant and insightful information. Think of it as a personalized learning feed, curated by the vast intelligence of the Internet. What makes this "hack" so effective is its proactive nature. You're not just passively waiting for opportunities to learn and grow; you're actively inviting them into your life. It's a testament to the power of leveraging technology to enhance our learning and growth. By staying informed and engaged, we can continuously refine our skills, expand our knowledge, and become more effective and impactful leaders.

AWARENESS

Honestly, even just the awareness developed via the data-gathering phases will carry you a long way toward Invested Leadership. Self-awareness is fundamental to Invested Leadership. Gathering data about our own behaviors, through journaling, feedback, or assessments, illuminates our strengths and weaknesses. This awareness sparks instinctive change and helps us recognize similar patterns in others, fostering empathy and understanding. Ultimately, this continuous cycle of self-reflection and awareness unlocks our potential for growth and allows us to become more effective leaders. Recognition leads to change.

CALL ON THE TEAM

Surround yourself with people whose strengths complement your own, who can fill in your potholes for you. For example, many leaders are simply incapable of (or don't see the value in) reading a room. Some leaders struggle to perceive subtle emotional cues like eye rolls or changes in tone, even when this blind spot is pointed out. They miss crucial nonverbal signals that reveal underlying feelings. This disconnect is problematic because power dynamics often prevent employees from expressing themselves candidly. Leaders who miss these cues risk misinterpreting situations, leading to poor decisions and decreased morale. Cultivating emotional intelligence and paying attention to nonverbal communication are essential for effective leadership.

The leader who considers social emotional cues such as these will not only be better able to care for those in the room but will gather valuable information. This is exactly the kind of pothole a principal can easily fill by finding someone on their team (or pulling someone in) who excels in this kind of emotional awareness.

Ultimately, this part of Invested Leadership is about recognizing the strength of the people around you and using those strengths to solve problems you can't solve on your own. Maybe you need someone who is really good at drawing people out, who has the patience to listen and pull out information. Maybe you want someone who's social and likes organizing and attending happy hours.

Say your employees want social gatherings, and you're an introvert who thinks office get-togethers are like razor blades in the eyes. If you force yourself to do karaoke, it will have the opposite of the intended effect. Fair or not, your employees will sense your misery and assume you don't care about them and are just going through the motions. That is so much worse than simply being honest about your introversion and discomfort in social scenarios. Instead of attending, you can explain that you recognize this need is important, which is why you've created a social committee or deputized someone on the leadership team to attend in your stead.

SOMETIMES WHAT PEOPLE NEED IS LESS ABOUT THE SPECIFIC ACT OF CARING AND MORE ABOUT FROM WHOM IT COMES.

That said, don't hand off every opportunity to demonstrate care to those in your charge. In such a scenario, everyone else on your leadership team will be growing but you. Share the labor when you need to, but don't share too much of it, or you abdicate leadership rather than exercise it. Worse, individual loyalties will develop toward others instead of you, and you could lose the locker room. If people see you trying, at the end of the day, they will respect that.

Anyway, sometimes care from the leader is specifically what's demanded. Sometimes what people need is less about the specific act of caring and more about from whom it comes. Ultimately, you are responsible for your people. If such a scenario overlaps with one of your potholes, do your best, and be honest about the challenge.

Partnering with other leaders in the delivery of care is a process. It can be difficult to define and quantify if only because it's going to look different in every context and at every point on the path of growth and change. If you're practicing Invested Leadership correctly, it won't be static—roles and duties will shift as well.

KEY TAKEAWAYS

- Be honest with yourself about your ability to care for those in your charge in each of the specific ways they require it. Don't force something inauthentic; it will backfire.
- Embrace the vulnerability inherent in working on yourself and allow others in the organization to hold you accountable. True strength is born of growth, not smoke and mirrors.
- When filling certain potholes yourself, allow recognition to lead to intuition and real change. Awareness is half the battle.
- Remember that you're not competing with other leaders but with the leader you were yesterday.
- Whenever you doubt your ability to authentically demonstrate care in a certain arena, lean on others in your leadership team to fill that pothole. This is itself a way of demonstrating care.
- But don't abdicate too much leadership or you'll lose the opportunity to grow (and the locker room).

"Talent wins games, but teamwork and intelligence win championships."

—MICHAEL JORDAN

"If you want to go fast, go alone. If you want to go far, go together."

—AFRICAN PROVERB

"The strength of the team is each individual member. The strength of each member is the team."

—PHIL JACKSON

"Teamwork is the ability to work together toward a common vision. The ability to direct individual accomplishments toward organizational objectives. It is the fuel that allows common people to attain uncommon results."

—ANDREW CARNEGIE

"Great things in business are never done by one person. They're done by a team of people."

—STEVE JOBS

"Alone we can do so little; together we can do so much."

—HELEN KELLER

CONCLUSION

Years ago, *Forbes* magazine ran an article about a specific practice exercised by business mogul Indra Nooyi, former CEO of PepsiCo. After positing the idea that people never stop caring what their parents think about them, she had an idea. She wrote letters to the parents of her direct reports, specifically citing why she thought each person was good at their job, what they had contributed to the organization, and why they were respected.

Nooyi is renowned for her emotional intelligence. She seeks out, listens to, and is genuinely affected by differing opinions. She's team oriented and has excelled at retaining talent. She is especially known for investing in her people. It's the way she was brought up in Pepsi, herself. Several leaders there mentored her and invested in her, developing her as a leader. Now, to get the best out of her people, she pays it forward. She has invested in people and cared for them, including, for example, by writing letters to parents.

Now, such an effort needs to be warranted and authentic, of course. Otherwise, the result will feel like when you get a birthday postcard from your optometrist. But when practiced with intention, such an effort can have profound results.

Hey, Eric here, jumping in personally to take over the narrative. When I saw that *Forbes* article, I was floored. Imagine the parents of a 50-something-year-old professional, probably in the C-suite, receiving a letter about their kid. It struck me as such a small and easy way to have a huge, authentic impact, to give meaning to people I care about. I decided to write letters that year for two of my colleagues. One of them was Stacie. Before Stacie was my partner, we were peers. Before that, for a time, she was my direct report.

Several years ago, at Christmas, I handed her a sealed letter. I explained that I didn't know what kind of baggage she might have with her parents, but that I had represented her in a positive light in this letter. If she was comfortable with that, I said, she could give me their address and I would mail it, or she could hand-deliver it to them.

* * *

Now it's Stacie, jumping in. My parents were local, and I was headed to their place within the next few days. I kept the envelope sealed and handed it to my mom first. Some background: I come from an Irish family that doesn't express much emotion. I could tell my mother was having a strong response because after she read it, she handed it to my dad and then hid in her bedroom rather than showing emotion in front of Dad and me. My dad was also moved by it, and then my mom came out of the bedroom and asked for it back because she wanted to read it again. That's when I realized how important the gesture was.

* * *

Let me give you a flavor of the letter (it's Eric again). Stacie, as a professional, has the reputation of being a bit of a hard-ass, a get-it-done kind of person. I happened to know another side of her. Years earlier, someone else in our organization, not even a direct report of Stacie's, received a cancer diagnosis. She was undergoing treatment in Charlotte, more than two hours away.

On weekends, Stacie would drive to sit with her while she received chemotherapy. No one else knew this was happening. When I found out, I was wildly impressed because, to be honest, I wouldn't have assumed that kind of behavior from her. I had not seen anything in the work environment that would lead me to believe she would sacrifice her own personal time to that degree. I wanted her parents to know they had raised someone of such high character. It took me 10 minutes to write it. And it helped develop such a strong loyalty between us that, years later, when I asked her to run Maestro with me, she agreed.

Organizations cannot succeed without loyalty. Loyalty is born of trust, and trust is born of care. A myriad of problems faced by businesses in the twenty-first century—at least as it relates to people—can all be mitigated by simple, human acts of recognition and care. This is not a new idea. Basic humanity was once the bedrock of hundreds of businesses across America, whether large or small. These businesses built a thriving economy that signaled the possibility of progress to the world.

CREATING CHANGE REALLY CAN BE AS SIMPLE AS STARTING CONVERSATIONS.

Somewhere along the way, humanity gave way to stock prices. Shareholders became more important than employees; those developments have had real deleterious ramifications. Workers feel disinterested, unengaged, and disgruntled. They feel adrift. No wonder they slack off, "quiet quit," or move on prematurely for seemingly greener pastures.

Many leaders today prioritize professionalism over personal connection, missing opportunities to build rapport and trust. This detachment creates a transactional workplace, wherein employees feel unseen. Simple conversations about personal interests can foster a sense of community and belonging, leading to greater engagement and productivity. It's time to rediscover the power of human connection in leadership. Invested Leadership is not a challenging proposition. It's rather straightforward. It merely requires effort and self-reflection.

We hope this book has outlined a simple, easy-to-follow plan for implementing real, organization-wide culture change. Take inventory of your strengths and weaknesses, and do the same for others in your organization. Learn from those in your charge how they want to be cared for.

Then find ways to demonstrate that care, whether personally or by leaning on the skillsets of other leaders. Iterate and repeat. Take over the world.

That's what will happen when you embark on the Invested Leadership journey. When a team of people makes its number one goal to care for one another, and everyone shares that mindset, the team is unstoppable. You build each other up by complementing rather than replicating one another. Case in point: the two of us have improved our leadership skills and professional careers immensely by caring for others in the workplace and doing so by complementing one another's skillsets.

Every step on the journey is a growth opportunity. It's common in corporate America to talk about growth opportunities stemming from, for example, a project gone wrong, or a client lost. Why don't we look at interpersonal evolution as the same kind of growth opportunity? After all, leadership doesn't only happen in a corporate setting. Neither should interpersonal growth occur only in other settings.

LEADERSHIP IS LIKE LANGUAGE: IT'S SPOKEN THE SAME WAY IN THE OFFICE, AT THE DINNER TABLE, AND IN CHURCH. IT'S NOT JUST A CORPORATE SKILL—IT'S A LIFE SKILL.

When you're working on yourself as a leader, you're doing so in all aspects of your life. Our friends and families also see us as leaders (and not just because we are a little bossy). We've shown over the years that we can take care of problems and help guide everyone through trying times. When you work to become a leader in the workplace, it expands out to being a leader in your life. You don't just walk out of the office and shut it off.

In that way, pursuing a leadership path—particularly the Invested Leadership path—is also a way of proving yourself across the board. When you set a goal as a leader to improve the lives of the people in your charge, you will do the same at home, with your friends, and even with strangers you meet. Leadership is like language: it's spoken the same way in the office, at the dinner table, and in church. It's not just a corporate skill—it's a life skill.

As we conclude this exploration of Invested Leadership, we urge you to reflect on the profound impact it can have on your organization and your own life. It's a philosophy centered on genuine care for your team's well-being and growth, fostering a culture where everyone feels valued, respected, and supported.

Invested Leaders are not distant figures; they actively participate in their team's development, offering guidance and support, especially during challenging times. They prioritize open communication and create a safe space for sharing ideas and feedback. It's about recognizing the unique needs and aspirations of each individual, empowering them to contribute their best work and reach their full potential.

Invested Leadership is not a passive approach; it demands self-awareness, empathy, and a willingness to adapt. It requires vulnerability and a commitment to personal growth, both for yourself and your team. It's a long-term commitment to building a culture of care and support, wherein everyone feels empowered to thrive.

We believe Invested Leadership is the key to unlocking a more humane, productive, and fulfilling workplace. It has the power to transform not only our organizations but also our lives. We invite you to embrace the principles of Invested Leadership. Nurture a workplace where everyone feels empowered to thrive. Together, we can build a better future for ourselves, our organizations, and the world around us.

Thank you for joining us on this journey. We hope this book has inspired you to become a more Invested Leader and cultivate a culture of care and support within your own spheres of influence. The culture of leadership you develop at work is also the culture of leadership you develop around you in life. In so doing, you make the world a slightly less toxic place, and you engender the same leadership skills in the next generation. Spread a culture of care throughout the world.

AFTERWORD

DON'T JUST TAKE OUR WORD FOR IT

"The best way to predict the future is to create it."

—PETER DRUCKER

"The greatest leader is not necessarily the one who does the greatest things. He is the one that gets the people to do the greatest things."

—RONALD REAGAN

"The leader has to be practical and a realist yet must talk the language of the visionary and the idealist."

—ERIC HOFFER

"A leader is one who knows the way, goes the way, and shows the way."

—JOHN C. MAXWELL

"Before you are a leader, success is all about growing yourself. When you become a leader, success is all about growing others."

—JACK WELCH

"A good leader takes a little more than his share of the blame, a little less than his share of the credit."

—ARNOLD GLASOW

"There are two ways of spreading light: to be the candle or the mirror that reflects it."

—EDITH WHARTON

"Leadership is the capacity to translate vision into reality."

—WARREN BENNIS

"The key to successful leadership today is influence, not authority."

—KEN BLANCHARD

"The best executive is the one who has sense enough to pick good [people] to do what he wants done, and self-restraint enough to keep from meddling with them while they do it."

—THEODORE ROOSEVELT

"Leadership is solving problems. The day soldiers stop bringing you their problems is the day you have stopped leading them. They have either lost confidence that you can help or concluded you do not care. Either case is a failure of leadership."

—COLIN POWELL

"Great leaders are almost always great simplifiers, who can cut through argument, debate, and doubt to offer a solution everybody can understand."

—COLIN POWELL

"Lead me, follow me, or get out of my way."

—GENERAL GEORGE PATTON

"Do not lead by hitting people over the head—that's assault, not leadership."

—DWIGHT D. EISENHOWER

"The supreme quality of leadership is integrity."

—DWIGHT D. EISENHOWER

"You don't lead by pointing and telling people some place to go. You lead by going to that place and making a case."

—KEN KESEY

"When your work speaks for itself, don't interrupt."

—HENRY J. KAISER

"Effective leadership is not about making speeches or being liked; leadership is defined by results not attributes."

—PETER DRUCKER

"The task of the leader is to get his people from where they are to where they have not been."

—HENRY KISSINGER

"The difference between a boss and a leader: A boss says, 'Go!' A leader says, 'Let's go!'"

—ANONYMOUS

"The challenge of leadership is to be strong, but not rude; be kind, but not weak; be bold, but not a bully; be thoughtful, but not lazy; be humble, but not timid; be proud, but not arrogant; have humor, but without folly."

—JIM ROHN

"Leadership should be born out of the understanding of the needs of those who would be affected by it."

—MARIAN ANDERSON

"Leadership is the art of getting someone else to do something you want done because he wants to do it."

—DWIGHT D. EISENHOWER

"The buck stops here."

—HARRY S. TRUMAN

"I must follow the people. Am I not their leader?"

—BENJAMIN DISRAELI

"The price of greatness is responsibility."

—WINSTON CHURCHILL

"Nearly all men can stand adversity, but if you want to test a man's character, give him power."

—ABRAHAM LINCOLN

"A genuine leader is not a searcher for consensus but a molder of consensus."

—MARTIN LUTHER KING JR.

"A leader takes people where they want to go. A great leader takes people where they don't necessarily want to go, but ought to be."

—ROSALYNN CARTER

"The nation will find it very hard to look up to the leaders who are keeping their ears to the ground."

—WINSTON CHURCHILL

"True leadership stems from individuality that is honestly and sometimes imperfectly expressed...Leaders should strive for authenticity over perfection."

—SHERYL SANDBERG

"You manage things; you lead people."

—REAR ADMIRAL GRACE HOPPER

"The most dangerous leadership myth is that leaders are born, that there is a genetic factor to leadership. That's nonsense; in fact, the opposite is true. Leaders are made rather than born."

—WARREN BENNIS

"To handle yourself, use your head; to handle others, use your heart."

—ELEANOR ROOSEVELT

"Example is not the main thing in influencing others. It is the only thing."

—ALBERT SCHWEITZER

"The best way to find yourself is to lose yourself in the service of others."

—MAHATMA GANDHI

"The quality of a leader is reflected in the standards they set for themselves."

—RAY KROC

"Never doubt that a small group of thoughtful, committed citizens can change the world; indeed, it's the only thing that ever has."

—MARGARET MEAD

"The only person you are destined to become is the person you decide to be."

—RALPH WALDO EMERSON

"The journey of a thousand miles begins with a single step."

—LAO TZU

"The best and most beautiful things in the world cannot be seen or even touched—they must be felt with the heart."

—HELEN KELLER

"The best way to cheer yourself up is to try to cheer somebody else up."

—MARK TWAIN

"The best way to predict your future is to create it."

—ABRAHAM LINCOLN

"The man who moves a mountain begins by carrying away small stones."

—CONFUCIUS

"The man who has confidence in himself gains the confidence of others."

—HASIDIC PROVERB

"The two most important days in your life are the day you are born and the day you find out why."

—MARK TWAIN

"The woman who follows the crowd will usually go no further than the crowd. The woman who walks alone is likely to find herself in places no one has ever been before."

—ALBERT EINSTEIN

"The most effective way to do it, is to do it."

—AMELIA EARHART

"The real opportunity for success lies within the person and not in the job."

—ZIG ZIGLAR

"The greatest discovery of all time is that a person can change his future by merely changing his attitude."

—OPRAH WINFREY

ACKNOWLEDGMENTS

Thank you to our families, friends, colleagues, direct reports, and all who have believed in us. Thank you to the excellent leaders from whose examples we've learned and to the bad "leaders" who drove us to strive for a better way.

AUTHOR BIOS

ERIC SANCHEZ, Managing Partner of Maestro Strategic Partners, empowers organizations to enhance their efficiency, innovation, and culture. Eric's experience spans law and technology. He was integral to a case that resulted in a $1.25 billion settlement and an invitation to the White House. He also designed legal software, resulting in nearly thirty patents. Eric is a veteran of the US Marine Corps and a graduate of Northwestern University.

For twenty-five years, STACIE MONAHAN served as a senior executive with a large law firm and within the insurance industry. A partner at Maestro Strategic Partners and in-demand consultant, Stacie specializes in system management and design. Renowned for her high level of emotional intelligence, she also has a track record of developing, mentoring, and empowering emerging leaders.